D1590136

Ian Steedman

Marx after Sraffa

© NLB, 1977

Second impression December 1978

NLB, 7 Carlisle Street, London W1

Designed by Ruth Prentice

Filmset by Servis Filmsetting Ltd,
Manchester

Printed in Great Britain by
Lowe & Brydone Printers Limited, Thetford, Norfolk

Bound by Kemp Hall Bindery, Oxford

ISBN 902308 49 1

Contents

A generalization
Fixed capital
Conclusion

To Ruth and Alison

Acknowledgements

I should like to thank P. Anderson, J. Eatwell, D. Elson, N. Geras and D. Purdy for extensive and extremely helpful discussions around various drafts of this work. Comments were also received from R. Blackburn, P. Devine, L. Harris, G. Hodgson, M. Morishima and R. Rowthorn and are gratefully acknowledged. Whilst the aforenamed are indeed responsible for the absence of various flaws from the following work, they bear no responsibility for those that remain.

In chapters 2, 3, 5, 9, 10 and 11, I have drawn, more or less freely, on previously published work and I should like to thank *Australian Economic Papers*, the *Conference of Socialist Economists*, *New Left Review* and the *Economic Journal* for permitting me to do so.

I am indebted to both Thordis Stephenson and Miss Edith Gillet and her colleagues for the production of an excellent typescript.

I.S.
June 1977

1

Principal Issues and Underlying Assumptions

Sraffa's book *Production of Commodities by Means of Commodities*, first published in 1960, had a quite precise purpose, indicated by its sub-title, Prelude to a Critique of Economic Theory. That purpose was to lay the foundation for the criticism of marginalist theories of wages, profits, rents and prices, a criticism which has now been carried out successfully. It was necessary for Sraffa to consider only a very restricted, albeit crucial, set of issues in economic theory; his central concern was with the relationships which necessarily hold between wages, profits and prices, for given conditions of production, when the wage rate, the rate of profit and the price of each commodity are uniform throughout the economy.[1] He was then able to examine the dependence of prices, of the 'value of capital' and of the choice between alternative methods of production on income distribution and hence to lay the required basis for the critique of marginalist theory.

The relations between wages, profits, prices and conditions of production,[2] to which Sraffa drew attention so sharply, were quickly seen to provide a foundation not only for the criticism of marginalist theory but also for the simple, definitive solution of certain issues

---

[1] Sraffa considers only 'prices of production', his book containing no reference to market prices; cf. Sraffa, *op. cit.*, Cambridge, 1960, p. 9. The same is true of the present work.

[2] No further reference will be made to rent, since rent and land will not be discussed here.

13

which had long been debated by Marxists.[3] The issues in question, while far from exhausting the entire content of Marx's political economy, are not insignificant ones and their definitive solution should have been welcomed by *all* those working to develop the materialist account of capitalist society. It was not.

The issues involved

While it would not be appropriate to set out the relevant issues in detail at this point – for to do that is precisely the function of this work – they may be summarized as follows, it being understood that the various qualifications and explanations needed will be considered below.

On the basis of certain common, reasonable assumptions it may be shown that:

i) the conditions of production and the real wage paid to workers, both specified in terms of physical quantities of commodities, suffice to determine the rate of profit (and less importantly, all prices of production);

ii) the quantities of labour embodied in the various commodities,[4] which can themselves only be determined once the conditions of production are known, thus play *no essential role* in the determination of the rate of profit (or of the prices of production);

iii) Marx's solution of the 'transformation problem' is incorrect, not only with respect to prices of production but also, more importantly, with respect to the rate of profit. The rate of profit in a competitive, capitalist economy is not equal, in general, to $[S/(C+V)]$, where S, C and V are aggregate surplus value, constant capital and variable capital respectively. Indeed, since the profit rate and all prices of production can be determined without reference to any value magnitude, the 'transformation problem' is a pseudo-problem, a

---

[3] It should be noted that Sraffa's *Production of Commodities by Means of Commodities* presents *no* criticisms of Marx.

[4] See below, pp. 19–20 and pp. 208 ff, for discussion of the relation between 'embodied labour-time' and Marx's concept of 'value'.

chimera; there *is no* problem of deriving profits from surplus value and production prices from values to be solved;

iv) the social allocation of labour power can be determined without reference to any value magnitude;

v) the relationship between surplus labour and the existence of profits can be established quite independently of Marx's concept of value;

vi) there is no *a priori* basis for establishing any expectation concerning the long-run movement of the rate of profit.

The significance of these issues

Marx, like other great theorists, regarded the analysis of the rate of profit as central to a coherent understanding of the workings of a capitalist economy. He saw the rate of profit as being the primary manifestation of surplus labour specific to capitalism; inevitably, then, he devoted much effort both to the criticism of earlier theories of the profit rate and to the development of his own theory. In that development he strove constantly to relate the rate of profit to value magnitudes. Consequently, the demonstration that the rate of profit, the prices of production and the social allocation of labour power can all be determined without *any* reference to value magnitudes raises questions which are fundamental to the appraisal of Marx's whole project.

To say this is not, of course, to reduce Marx's theory to these particular issues; his scope was far wider. The fact remains, nevertheless, that these issues are crucial within Marx's theory – and were known to be so by Marx. To attempt to sidestep them by suggesting that they are marginal issues, or that they belong to a non-Marxist frame of discourse, or that they are mere details without significance for Marx's major work would be to demean Marx, not to defend him. Marx showed only contempt for those who sought to evade the ruthless criticism of ideas; no-one can 'defend' Marx by refusing to follow him in this regard.[5]

[5] To suggest that Marx would not have been concerned with 'mere details of logic' would, of course, be both false and demeaning.

16

Underlying assumptions
It will be as well to set out here the underlying assumptions which are to be *taken as read* in the following chapters, which establish, in detail, the above mentioned (and other) findings. These general premises will not be repeated chapter by chapter.

Capitalist commodity economies
The only economies considered are commodity economies, in which all products are produced for exchange and in which production and the allocation of labour power between industries are co-ordinated solely through the market.[6]

More specifically, the only economies considered are fully developed, capitalist commodity economies, in which all production activities are organized and controlled by capitalists (or their agents); production is driven exclusively by the search for profit. All produced means of production are owned by the capitalists, whose money capital is mobile between industries. This mobility of money capital constantly tends to produce a uniform rate of profit.

All labour is performed by workers, characterized by their familiar 'double freedom', the freedom *to* offer their labour power to which ever capitalist they choose and the freedom *from* ownership of any land or produced means of production. Workers are thus freely mobile between industries but the only thing they have to sell is their capacity to work.

It need hardly be said that the object of discussion is thus an 'abstract' capitalist economy.

Production
As has already been stated, all production is assumed to be carried out by workers, in a socialized labour process under the direction

[6] Non-reproducible goods will not be discussed, whether they be land, minerals or 'oil-paintings by Rembrandt'.

and control of the capitalists (or their agents), using produced means of production and producing products all of which are the property of the capitalists. That the production process is thus a social process and that the process is initiated and controlled for the sole purpose of making profits does not, of course, alter the fact that the physical inputs, the labour done and the physical outputs produced stand in certain necessary relations to one another. The following analyses will generally start from such conditions of production.

It should be noted carefully that the procedure of starting an analysis from relations between physically specified inputs, amounts of labour-time and physically specified outputs has the following (negative) properties:

i) it does not involve a denial of the social nature of the capitalist production process;

ii) it does not involve a denial that coercion is exercised and resisted in the capitalist production process (indeed it can be used to analyse these phenomena – see chapter 6);

iii) it does not imply that the conditions of production applying in a given capitalist economy in a given period are independent of the economic, scientific, cultural and political history and situation of that economy, or of the 'balance of forces' between workers and capitalists in the workplace;

iv) it does not entail concern with use values and concrete labour to the exclusion of exchange value and abstract labour (all commodities will be seen below as *both* use values and exchange values and all labour will be seen as *both* concrete labour and abstract labour).

As will be seen in the sequel, when the object of discussion is, say, the relation between wages, profits and prices of production, the production relations will be 'frozen' and taken as determined exogenously; this merely amounts to assuming that the various determinants of production relations, including the shop-floor balance of forces, are (hypothetically) held constant. This does not, of course, mean that the role of those determinants is denied; it is merely a procedure for focusing attention on one problem at a time.

When, however, the object of discussion is, say, the effect of speed-up in the labour process or the effects of technical change on the rate of profit, those same production relations will, necessarily, be 'unfrozen'.

These procedural remarks should help to explain the treatment of 'labour power' in the text which follows. Whenever the workplace balance of forces is held 'frozen', because that balance is not the immediate object of enquiry, the purchase of a given capacity to work, at a given wage, *will* lead to the performance of a given amount of labour. The conceptual distinction between 'labour power' and 'labour', of course, remains but its importance lapses, provisionally, under the given assumptions. *That* is why the distinction is often not emphasized below. It is not, however, rejected and will, indeed, be employed when it has force, for example in discussing variations in the working day, the speed and intensity of work, and so on.

There will, no doubt, be some who will continue to insist that it is 'unMarxist' ever to take conditions of production as the starting point of one's analysis.[7] Marx, it need hardly be said, had more sense, as the following testifies:

'The fact that the production of use-values, or goods, is carried on under the control of a capitalist and on his behalf does not alter the general character of that production. We shall therefore, in the first place, have to consider the labour process independently of any specific social formation.'[8]

Reproduction
The capitalist economies considered are always in a self-reproducing state, whether the reproduction be 'simple' or 'expanded' (stationary or growing), so that production, exchange and distribution are

---

[7] Only those with the shortest memories can be unaware of the dangers of attempting to 'deal' with arguments by labelling them 'unMarxist'.

[8] Karl Marx, *Capital*, vol. I, Penguin/NLR edition, 1976, p. 283. See, more generally on this point, *ibid.*, chapter 7, 'The Labour Process and the Valorization Process' and the Appendix, 'Results of the Immediate Process of Production'.

always considered as a unity. Since capitalists will remain capitalists and workers remain workers, the social relations of production are reproduced, as well as the means of production.

For the most part, reproduction will be taken to be 'simple'. The reason for this is not, of course, that simple reproduction is typical of capitalist systems; it is that many of the questions discussed below do not depend on the nature of the reproduction involved, so that it is obviously sensible to consider them in the context of the 'simple' case.

Labour-time, value, money and price
Unless otherwise stated, all labour is taken to be unskilled, 'simple' labour, all labour being of equal ability and equal 'intensity'. Any worker can perform every kind of 'concrete' labour. All productive activities of a given kind are assumed to be carried out under identical conditions and with equal efficiency, so that each individual expenditure of labour-time is an expenditure of socially necessary labour-time. The impossible task of adding together quantities of different concrete labour-times will not be attempted, it may be noted![9] All summations of labour-times are summations of quantities of abstract labour.

It is to be taken as read throughout that the exchange of commodities takes place via the medium of money. That money will seldom be referred to explicitly, and that the functions of money

[9] Gerstein (see footnote 13) actually makes the mistake of asserting that abstract labour, as such, never appears in the Sraffa-based critique, which, he says, considers only concrete labour. This assertion could hardly be more wide of the mark. As will be seen in later chapters, the total labour-time embodied in, say, a car, is represented as the sum of the labour-time spent in assembling the car, that spent in making the steel, etc., used by car workers, that spent in producing iron ore, coal, electricity and so on for use in making the steel, etc., etc. The *very fact* that these different labour-times, expended in a capitalist economy, are added together means that they are treated as abstract labour-time. (One can no more add 7 hours of *concrete* coal-mining labour to 3 hours of *concrete* tea-making labour than one can add 7 apples to 3 oranges.) Cf., Marx, *op. cit.*, p. 296.

other than the medium of exchange function are not discussed, is to be attributed to the fact that the (obviously very important) issues of crises, 'effective demand', 'Say's Law' and so on are abstracted from, reproduction being assumed to take place smoothly.

The foregoing assumptions entail that the magnitude of value is a quantity of embodied labour-time. *This will often be abbreviated* to the statement that 'value equals embodied labour-time' (an abbreviation used by Marx). It will be clear to the serious reader that, since only capitalist commodity economies are considered, this abridgement involves no denial of Marx's statements concerning the 'form of value', abstract social labour, the 'universal equivalent' and so on.

The prices considered throughout this work are always prices of production, for market prices are never considered. It should, perhaps, be remarked that, by definition, prices of production are the prices which would obtain in the (hypothetical) presence of a uniform rate of profit: the concepts of a uniform rate of profit and of prices of production are indissolubly related. It is for this reason, and *not* because the determination of prices of production is a major theoretical concern in its own right, that prices of production will appear frequently in the sequel. If one is concerned to explain the rate of profit then, *ipso facto*, one must be concerned with prices of production.[10]

Wages

Wages are treated in this work, as they were by Marx, as being exogenously determined, in terms of a specified bundle of commodities, in a given economy in a given period. Naturally, one does not thereby deny that wages are socially determined or that they change over time. (It should go without saying that to assume an

---

[10] The (supposedly rhetorical) question 'Who is interested in prices? That can be left to bourgeois theory' thus simply embodies a confusion. The answer to the question is '*Anyone* concerned to provide a serious theory of the rate of profit, in particular, and of the laws of motion of capitalism, in general'.

exogenously given wage is *not* to assume a wage providing only a biological subsistence level of living.)

At some points in the following chapters the wage is taken to be paid in advance; in others it is assumed to be paid *ex post*, at the end of the cycle of production. It is to be noted with care that the varying choice of assumption is dictated purely by the resulting convenience for the analysis in hand. Nothing will be said, on the basis of either assumption, which could not also be said, *mutatis mutandis*, using the other assumption and any reader who feels (incorrectly) that the choice between these assumptions is important can always make the appropriate change in assumption; no essential change will result in the conclusions, provided that they are correctly drawn.[11]

The obscurantist response

The response of many Marxists to the kind of results presented in this book has been not to *face* them but to *obscure* them, not to consider their validity or implications but to ignore them and to 'justify' this response by merely asserting (correctly) that Marx was concerned with wider issues. It should be transparently clear that from this (correct) assertion *nothing* follows concerning the validity of the various propositions in question. The obscurants often also allege (incorrectly) that those engaged in the derivation of such propositions either ignore or even deny many of Marx's essential insights. The usual basis for such allegations is the mere absence from the arguments involved of lengthy rehearsals of Marx's basic

---

[11] Gerstein (see footnote 13) pp. 276, 278, asserts that the assumption that wages are paid *ex post* involves 'ideological bias' and the view that workers and capitalists 'share' the net product. In fact, of course, if wages are taken as given, no question of 'sharing' the net product arises, whether those wages are paid at the beginning or the end of the production period. This lapse provides a 'good' example of an emotional response to a simple but misunderstood point of reasoning. (Gerstein is also wrong to say, p. 275, 'There are, in general, n solutions for r. Presumably the largest is the one that corresponds to the actual rate of profit.' It is, of course, well-known that the *economically* relevant solution is actually the smallest of the mathematical solutions.)

22

ideas, as if one necessarily denied the truth of all those propositions whose truth one does not explicitly affirm! Such demands for the constant repetition of basic ideas perhaps indicate how shallow are the roots of the recent revival of Marxist culture.

As is to be expected, the different obscurants do not all make exactly the same allegations against the Marx-critique[12] based on the work of Sraffa but it is not difficult to construct from their writings a `composite allegation', which encompasses all the most common, specific complaints. [13] [14]

The composite allegation

The type of argument exemplified in the present text is flawed (it is alleged) by the following – in some cases interconnected – `failures'.
a) It is asocial and ahistorical, failing to represent capitalism as a specific mode of production. In particular, relations of production are viewed in a purely `natural' (non-social) way and capital is not seen as a social relation (alternatively, is seen as a social relation only with respect to questions of distribution). The analysis is purely formal.
b) It is concerned only with exchange and distribution, paying little or no attention to the process of production.
c) In so far as production is considered, it is seen as a purely natural,

[12] The term `critique' is, of course, used here *not* in the sense of totally negative, dismissive criticism but rather to mean criticism leading to a new theory embodying the strengths of the old but shedding its weaknesses.
[13] The more responsible `defences' of Marx against the Sraffa-based critique include B. Fine and L. Harris, `Controversial Issues in Marxist Economic Theory' (in) *The Socialist Register*, London, 1976; I. Gerstein, `Production, Circulation and Value', *Economy and Society*, 1976 and R. B. Rowthorn, `Neo-Classicism, Neo-Ricardianism and Marxism', *New Left Review*, no. 86, 1974; see the first two of these three articles for extensive bibliographies, including references to all the various works from which the allegation has been composited.
[14] If I have omitted any important item from the composite allegation, the omission is not intended but is due to oversight.

technical matter, not as a social process. Even if social relations are considered with respect to distribution, they are not considered in the context of production.

d) The coercion, direction and control of the labour process by capitalists, or their agents, is not discussed; nor, therefore, is worker resistance to that coercion.

e) It does not deal with the dynamic of capitalism, with accumulation or with crises.

f) It is concerned only with quantitative matters, to the complete exclusion of qualitative issues. Thus 'value' is seen *merely* as embodied labour-time, the 'form of value' being entirely ignored. Marx's concepts of concrete labour, abstract labour, value and labour power are either misrepresented or are actually rejected.

g) The source, or 'origin', of profit is not explained and the concepts of surplus labour and surplus value are ignored or rejected.

The allegation is specious

To the reader familiar with Marx's work, the composite allegation presented above might well appear, if well-founded, to constitute a severe indictment of the Sraffa-based critique of Marx but it would be a paradox indeed if such a reader were content to consider only the superficial appearance of things. Careful consideration of the underlying assumptions set out above will show at once that some of the particular allegations are unfounded.

It has already been stated that the obscurants evade the issues involved rather than meet them head on; this may now be considered further in the context of the composite allegation. Suppose, purely for the sake of the argument, that allegations a), b), c), d), e) and f) *were fully justified* (which they are not). This would mean that the Sraffa-based critique of Marx is concerned only with a restricted, precisely defined range of issues (which may or may not have further ramifications), *saying nothing one way or the other* on most aspects of Marx's thought. *It would not mean that the arguments which are actually put forward in such a critique are false.*[15] This crucial fact is easily overlooked in the midst of lengthy disquisitions on the historicity of modes of production, the centrality of production as a social process, the unrelenting shop-floor struggle between workers and capitalists, the essentially dynamic nature of capitalism or the form of value. Such discourses may show that their authors have read Marx but they do *nothing* to meet the Sraffa-based critique of Marx.

More specifically, whatever the extent and the importance of Marx's treatment of the form of value, Marx did make *important* statements concerning embodied labour-time, the magnitude of value and the determination of the general rate of profit (and of prices of production). Some of those statements have been shown to be *false.* That fact cannot be altered – and ought not to be obscured – by incessant recitations of Marx's other views and statements, concerning the 'form of value' or anything else, or by (misleading) suggestions that the issues involved here are peripheral to Marx's work.

Similarly, the (correct) assertions that the Sraffa-based critique of Marx seldom refers *explicitly* to the concepts of concrete labour, abstract labour and labour power provide no basis for the (rational) rejection of that critique.

Element g) of the composite allegation has both an explicit and an implicit aspect. The explicit charge, that the Sraffa-based critique of Marx makes no reference to surplus labour or surplus value, is either quite simply false or is a variant on the charge that 'value' as understood by Marx is never fully discussed. The implicit aspect lies in the suggestion that Sraffa-based theories give only a 'superficial' explanation of the existence of profits in terms of distribution and

[15] This point is well-understood by some. Thus Rowthorn, in the article cited above, provides a forceful presentation of allegations a) to e). Yet being well-versed in the logical content of the relevant arguments, he at no point rejects any one of the conclusions reached in the Sraffa-based critique of Marx; he merely says that the scope of the arguments in question is limited. The point is perhaps less clearly taken by some of those who have quoted Rowthorn's paper.

exchange, while Marx's arguments provide an 'essential' or 'real' explanation in terms of production. The first half of this suggestion is only a variant of elements a) to e), considered above, while its second half is simply false, as will emerge from the following chapters.

[The issue of 'superficial' explanations perhaps deserves a further remark, which has a bearing on many aspects of the composite allegation, and which should be noted clearly. If it is said that, e.g., the rate of profit is determined by A, B and C, it is *always* possible to ask, 'Yes, but what determines A, B, and C?', that being so whatever are A, B and C. That question will always be legitimate, in some frame of reference, but it must not be taken to mean that the determination in terms of A, B and C *is invalid.* Many of the supposed 'defences' of Marx against the Sraffa-based critique have amounted to no more than the implicit denial of this simple truth.]

As a refutation of the Sraffa-based critique, the composite allegation and all of its elements are completely specious.[16] The resounding phrases and lofty themes, often found in such allegations, serve *only* to obscure the issues at hand. The Sraffa-based critique of Marx *cannot* be met head on and rationally rejected, for the simple reason that it is correct. Thus the self-appointed 'defenders' of Marx descend into evasion.

The issues involved, it is sad but true, have been the object of long and often fruitless debate: it is time to acknowledge that they can be resolved and to consider the further ramifications of that necessary resolution. There is no legitimate excuse for further evasion concerning the Sraffa-based critique of Marx: in particular, as has been set out at some length above, that critique cannot be airily dismissed

[16] Much less important than the question whether the Sraffa-based *critique* of Marx is open to the composite allegation (it is not) is the question whether the Sraffa-based *critics* of Marx have or have not been aware of the various issues raised (irrelevantly) by the obscurants. The appropriate evidence being largely anecdotal and circumstantial, the space necessary to show that they have generally been aware of these aspects of Marx's thought would be out of all proportion to the small importance of the question. I merely state that I have always been so aware.

26

as belonging to a different frame of discourse.[17] The Sraffa-based results are not only correct but derive from arguments which *do no* depend on ignoring or rejecting Marx's basic materialist frame work.[18] Furthermore, they relate not to marginal but to centra issues in Marx's theory; as was remarked above, Marx was himsel well aware of the importance of a sound theory of the rate of profit (and prices of production) for the proper understanding of a capital ist economy and its development. The *appropriate* response of Marxists to the Sraffa-based critique of Marx is thus not to evade it or obscure it but to grasp it, to absorb it and to use it in the con struction of an improved theory of the capitalist economy.

The structure of the present work

Chapters 2 to 5 below present alternative discussions of the under lying issue of the determination of the rate of profit in a capitalist economy; it is shown in varied ways and at various levels of gener ality that no value magnitude plays any essential role in that determination. Each of these chapters is based on the simplifying assumptions that only circulating capital is used and that no pure joint products are produced. The same assumptions are adopted in chapters 6 to 8, which deal with a number of extensions to the arguments of chapters 2 to 5, showing how variations within the

[17] It is incumbent on those who would seek to evade the Sraffa-based critique by such a move to show just how their *precisely stated* definitions and assumptions are both such as to assist one's understanding of capitalism and not such as to be open to the Sraffa-based critique.

[18] Nothing has been, or will be said here concerning Marx's work on commodity fetishism, reification and related issues. It may well be that *creative* thinkers, inspired by Marx's work on these matters, will produce further insights into the nature of capitalist societies. One can be confident, however, that such creative work will derive no inspiration whatsoever from the mere repetition, often in language far less compelling than that of the original, of what Marx wrote. It may be noted that Marx's ideas in this field bear *no intrinsic* relation to the questions whether production prices are determined by values, whether profit equals surplus value, and so on. They relate rather to certain features of the capitalist commodity producing economy which are taken as read throughout this work.

.bour process, heterogeneous labour, differential wages, certain
urnover problems, etc., may be treated within the 'physical quan-
ties' framework of analysis advocated throughout this book. After
discussion of the 'falling rate of profit' in chapter 9, attention is
urned, in chapters 10 to 13, to the analysis of fixed capital using (and
»int product producing) capitalist economies. Whilst certain addi-
onal complexities naturally arise with the introduction of fixed
ipital, etc., it is shown that the central findings of the simpler
nalyses of chapters 2 to 8 are little affected; under simple, reasonable
ssumptions, the physical conditions of production and real wages
iffice to determine the rate of profit, all prices of production, which
iethods of production are used, at what age machines are scrapped,
ie social allocation of labour power, and so on. *No* value magnitude
of the slightest relevance to that determination. It will be con-
uded, therefore, that Marx's value magnitude reasoning should be
bandoned by those working to develop the materialist account of
ie capitalist economy.

No claim to significant originality is made for the arguments
resented below. On the contrary, the far more significant claim –
iat the arguments given below are correct – is buttressed by the fact
iat many of the results presented here have been obtained by
arious writers.[19] The objective of the book is to present well-

---

[19] See, for example,
1. G. Abraham-Frois et E. Berrebi. *Théorie de la Valeur, des Prix et de l'Accumulation*, Paris, 1976.
2. L. von Bortkiewicz. 'Value and Price in the Marxian System', *International Economic Papers*, 1952. (This is an English translation of the second and third parts of a three part article originally published, in German, in 1906/1907.)
3. A. Bródy. *Prices, Proportions and Planning, A Mathematical Restatement of the Labour Theory of Value*, Amsterdam, 1970.
4. V. K. Dmitriev. *Economic Essays on Value, Competition and Utility*, Cambridge, 1974. (The first essay, which is the one relevant to the present work, was first published, in Russian, in 1898.)
5. P. Garegnani. *Il Capitale nelle Teorie della Distribuzione*, Milano, 1960.
6. M. Lippi. *Marx: il Valore come Costo Sociale Reale*, Milano, 1976.

established results in a coherent and (as far as possible) simple way,[20] emphasizing that arguments entirely consistent with Marx's materialist analysis both provide answers to some of the important questions with which Marx grappled and show that his value magnitude analysis is irrelevant to those answers.

---

7. M. Morishima, *Marx's Economics. A Dual Theory of Value and Growth*, Cambridge, 1973.
8. M. Morishima. 'Marx in the Light of Modern Economic Theory'. *Econometrica*, 1974.
9. N. Okishio. 'A Mathematical Note on Marxian Theorems'. *Weltwirtschaftliches Archiv*, 1963.

It might be wondered whether 'Marx after Dmitriev' or 'Marx after Bort-kiewicz' might not be a proper title for the present work but Sraffa's work has proved to mark a turning point, by providing a rigorous framework of analysis within which the pioneering works of Dmitriev and Bortkiewicz become (important) special cases.

[20] Mathematical arguments have, as far as possible, been preceded by simple numerical examples; the mathematical 'level' of the argument is thus oscillatory, not ever increasing, and the reader who finds a particular section difficult is therefore encouraged to press forward. Since any attempt to satisfy *both* mathematical and non-mathematical readers is doomed to failure, I have steered towards the interest of the latter; to the former, who might have pre-ferred a less informal argument in certain passages, I can only apologize and swear on oath that the informality does not reflect any contempt for rigorous argument! It may also be noted here that with respect to those chapters which are based on previously published papers, no attempt has been made to polish away every element of repetition or difference of emphasis.

2

The 'Transformation Problem'

Marxist economists have wasted much time and energy in the discussion of an intrinsically unimportant problem, the so-called 'transformation problem'. While the question is not really of great interest, it must nevertheless be sorted out, not least to end the waste of time of Marxist economists. The purpose of this chapter is to pose some of the central points as starkly as possible, making no use of arithmetic or algebraic arguments. Subsequent chapters will provide more detailed discussion.

Marx's 'solution' is logically inconsistent

As is well-known, Marx's 'solution' to the transformation problem can be found in *Capital*, vol. III, in *Theories of Surplus Value*, Part II, and in a letter, to Engels, of August 2nd, 1862. A minor problem with Marx's 'solution' is that he failed to transform the prices of inputs (see below) but this is easily dealt with and is not the central objection to Marx's approach. The central objection is that, even if input prices are transformed, Marx's 'solution' is *internally inconsistent*.

It may be worthwhile to state at some length why Marx's 'solution' is internally inconsistent. In a given economy (in a given year) there will be a bundle of commodities going to the capitalists (which constitute net investment and capitalists' consumption), a bundle of commodities which replace produced means of production (the physical aspect of constant capital) and a bundle of commodities going to workers as wages (the physical aspect of variable capital). In order to form a rate of profit it is clear that one must 'value' these three bundles in a consistent way. Marx 'values' them in terms of embodied labour, to obtain aggregate surplus value S, constant capital C and variable capital V, and then defines the rate of profit *in value terms* as $S/(C+V)$. To obtain the rate of profit *in money terms*, however, one must 'value' the three bundles in terms of prices and then divide profit by total capital.[1]

If all prices were proportional to values, i.e. to quantities of embodied labour, then, it will be clear, the two rates of profit (in value terms and in money terms) would be the same. In general, however, the two rates of profit must differ once prices diverge from values, *which is precisely the situation that Marx was concerned with*.

Now if these two profit rates differ, which is the significant one? Which will affect capitalists' decisions and actions? And which will tend to be made uniform, as between industries, in a competitive economy? The answer is self-evident; it is the money rate of profit which affects decisions and tends to be equalized. The 'value rate of profit', used by Marx, is of no concern to capitalists, it is unknown to capitalists and there is no force acting to make it equal as between industries. The implication is clear; $S/(C+V)$ is *not* a significant rate of profit in a capitalist economy, and it does *not* equal the actual, money, rate of profit. Furthermore, one cannot assume that it will be a 'close approximation' to the actual rate of profit; one can easily construct sensible numerical examples in which $S/(C+V)$ is very different from the rate of profit.[2] It is also easy to construct examples of two economies having the same V and the same S but different C's, such that the economy with the higher C, and hence the *lower* $S/(C+V)$, has the *higher* money rate of profit. Thus even the ranking of economies by $S/(C+V)$ can differ from their ranking by the

---

[1] Since we are concerned here only with the *ratio* of profits in terms of prices to capital in terms of prices, it clearly does not matter what standard of prices is adopted, since the *ratio* will be independent of the standard chosen.

[2] See, e.g., chapter 3.

profit rate.

Marx's argument, then, is internally inconsistent. He assumes that $S/(C + V)$ is the rate of profit but then derives the result that prices diverge from values, which means precisely, in general, that $S/(C + V)$ is *not* the rate of profit.

The above criticism, it may be noted, is quite independent of the question whether or not input prices should be transformed (see below). Even more important to notice is the fact that adherents to Marx's 'solution' never attempt a *direct reply* to the above criticism. The reason for this is simple; the criticism is sound and cannot be answered.

Transformation of input prices

It was stated above that a minor problem with Marx's solution is that he failed to transform input prices. It has occasionally been argued, however, that this is no problem at all and that it is quite proper not to transform input prices. Two points need to be made; first that input prices do have to be transformed in any sensible solution and second that Marx was fully aware of that fact.

That input prices have to be transformed follows quite simply from the fact that all capitalists take decisions in price terms, purchase their inputs at money prices and strive to maximize the money rate of profit. A 'theoretical system' in which a given commodity has different prices according to whether it is being sold or being purchased just does not correspond to *any* real capitalist economy. If we do not transform input prices then we commit the absurdity of assuming that the price paid for a commodity by the immediate purchaser can differ from the price received by the immediate seller!

That input prices must be transformed in any sensible solution is clear. No less clear is the fact that Marx was perfectly well aware of this, even though he failed to take account of it in the solutions he left (in unfinished manuscripts and a letter, it must be remembered).

The following three passages from *Capital*, vol. III, Part II, will

32

suffice to show that Marx was well aware that input prices must be transformed.[3]

i) '. . . the fact that under capitalist production the elements of productive capital are, as a rule, bought on the market, and that for this reason their prices include profit which has already been realised, hence, include the price of production of the respective branch of industry together with the profit contained in it, so that profit of one branch of industry goes into the cost-price of another.' (P. 160.)

(Marx goes on to argue, incorrectly, that in aggregate this makes no difference but that does not affect our point here.)

ii) 'We had originally assumed that the cost-price of a commodity equalled the *value* of the commodities consumed in its production. But for the buyer the price of production of a specific commodity is its cost-price, and may thus pass as cost-price into the prices of other commodities. Since the price of production may differ from the value of a commodity, it follows that the cost-price of a commodity containing this price of production of another commodity may also stand above or below that portion of its total value derived from the value of the means of production consumed by it. It is necessary to remember this modified significance of the cost-price, and to bear in mind that there is always the possibility of an error if the cost-price of a commodity in any particular sphere is identified with the value of the means of production consumed by it.' (Pp. 164–5, italics in original.)

iii) 'We have seen how a deviation in prices of production from values arises from:

1) adding the average profit instead of the surplus-value contained in a commodity to its cost-price;

2) the price of production, which so deviates from the value of a commodity, entering into the cost price of other commodities as one of its elements, so that the cost-price of a commodity may already contain a deviation from value in those means of production con-

---

[3] Page references are to the Moscow, 1966 edition.

sumed by it, quite aside from a deviation of its own which may arise through a difference between the average profit and the surplus-value.' (Pp. 206–7.)

It is beyond comprehension that anyone should attribute to Marx the idea that it is wrong to transform input prices.

Alternative solutions

As is well-known, such writers as Dmitriev, v. Bortkiewicz and Sraffa have presented solutions to the question of what profit rate and prices of production will rule in an economy, with a given wage and given conditions of production. These solutions are internally consistent, they are quite simple to understand (especially the Dmitriev and v. Bortkiewicz solutions)[4] and they show that profit rates and prices depend on real wages and on production conditions, just the things that Marx emphasized. These solutions are well-known and we need only note two points here. First, these solutions, unlike that of Marx, are logically coherent. Second, that those who oppose such solutions *never* attempt any direct logical criticism of them. Instead they attempt to dismiss them by a process of derogatory labelling, by implying (incorrectly) that the acceptance of such solutions leads inexorably to the acceptance of subjective value theory or by merely asserting that solutions making profit different from surplus value *must* be unacceptable (see below). This kind of 'non-argument' cannot be allowed currency any longer. No-one has presented a direct logical criticism of these solutions and that for the simple reason that there is no *logical* criticism to be made. So far as they go, these solutions *are* logically sound – and that is that.

The above does not, of course, prevent one from saying that these solutions do not go far enough. The point has been made, for example, that equilibrium solutions are only a first step and that a theory of disequilibrium profits and prices needs to be developed. This is certainly so and needs to be said but it must not be allowed to

---

[4] *Cf.*, chapter 5 below.

obscure the point that on the first step of equilibrium solutions, Marx's is just wrong while the others are correct. Furthermore, there is no reason at all to expect that Marx's 'solution' can be developed into a dynamic theory; an approach which fails the simpler test is not likely to meet the harder one.

Why are people afraid of the alternative solutions?
Why is it that some Marxist economists shy away from the fact that Marx's 'solution' is incoherent, while the alternative solutions are perfectly logical, and ignore the direct, logical criticisms of the former, shutting their eyes to the fact that they have no direct, logical criticism to make of the latter? One major reason (there may be others) is, perhaps, the following.

If one adopts Marx's 'solution' then it follows inevitably both that total price equals total value and that total profit equals total surplus value. The latter equality may *appear* to give strength to the view that profit is simply surplus value allocated in a certain way and that exploitation is thus the source of profit, the latter not being the result of 'profit on alienation' or any other process in the sphere of circulation.

If, on the other hand, one adopts one of the logically coherent solutions then, in general, one finds that neither the total price/total value nor the total profit/total surplus value equality will hold. One hypothesis is that people are afraid of these coherent solutions because they fear that if total profit can diverge from total surplus value then the way is open to theories attributing the existence of profits to circulation processes, 'contributions' made by capitalists, etc. *This fear is completely unjustified.* It is simple, within these alternative solutions, to show how profits will be positive *if and only if* there is surplus value, i.e. capitalist exploitation. That is all that is at issue; any question of total profit and total surplus value being equal in *magnitude* is trivial.

The alternative, and coherent, solutions do not undermine the idea that exploitation is the source of profit; on the contrary, they provide a simple means of demonstrating how the existence of surplus value is a necessary and sufficient condition for the existence of profit. Indeed the alternative solutions bring to light the fact that the determinants of the profit rate are precisely the determinants of the rate of surplus value, which Marx analysed so intensively in *Capital*, vol. I, namely the daily wage, the length of the working day and the conditions of production of wage commodities. (We mean, of course, conditions of direct *and* indirect production of wage commodities.) Thus these approaches mesh the analyses of rate of surplus value and rate of profit more closely together than Marx was able to do. Marx's (incorrect) approach appears to show that the rate of profit depends on the *use* which capitalists make of surplus value (i.e. which commodities they produce for their own consumption and investment) and not only on the conditions of production of surplus. The alternative (correct) approaches show that this is not so; the rate of profit depends on the conditions of production of surplus value and *not* on the use made of that surplus, which is precisely the conclusion most consonant with an analysis emphasizing production.

That these formal solutions take as given the real wage and the conditions of its production must not be misinterpreted to mean that they are asocial, ahistorical solutions; it means only that they form merely one part of a full analysis. One is perfectly free to go further and analyse the social, historical, factory-floor and political determinants of the real wage and of production conditions. Indeed, one is precisely in a better position to do this properly once one has adopted a coherent solution to the 'transformation problem', for such a solution shows which factors affect the rate of profit and prices of production and which do not.

Conclusion

The 'solution' of the transformation problem offered by Marx is quite unacceptable; it is internally incoherent, even when input prices are transformed. Alternative and coherent solutions exist which, in their own, limited, terms are perfectly acceptable. They are logically sound and they can be used to make a basic Marxist point; capitalist exploitation is the source of profit. Marxist economists should stop wasting their time in incompetent debates on simple matters of logic. When they have freed themselves from the incubus of the 'transformation problem' they will perhaps be able to devote their energies to worthwhile Marxist theoretical work.

3

Value, Price and Profit

In *Capital*, vol. I, Marx set out his theory of value and exploitation and showed, through his concept of the value of labour power, how 'freedom' of exchange is quite compatible with exploitation and the existence of surplus value. His argument was both strengthened and simplified by the assumption that commodities exchange at value. In Volume III Marx turned to the more detailed question of how the profit rate and production prices are determined when the value composition of capital differs between industries and consequently commodities do not exchange at value. He was anxious to stress the idea that fundamentally profits and prices were just 'transformed' value quantities, so that the essence of the Volume I argument was unaffected by the Volume III complications. Over the last 15 years or so, academic economics has generated a considerable discussion of questions which bear directly on Marx's treatment of the relations between wages, profits, values and prices: relations which are clearly of importance for Marxist analyses of many issues in political economy.[1] The purpose of this chapter is to set out, by means of a simple numerical example, some of the conclusions which can be drawn concerning Marx's analysis of the relations between values, prices and profits. A more general discussion will be presented in the next chapter.

[1] Much of this discussion was provoked by Piero Sraffa's *Production of Commodities by Means of Commodities*, Cambridge, 1960; for a non-technical review see Joan Robinson, 'Piero Sraffa and the Rate of Exploitation', *New Left Review*, no. 31, 1965.

The methods of production and the real wage

Marx normally described the economy in terms of value quantities, such as C(constant capital), V(variable capital), S(surplus value) and W(total value of gross output). These value quantities, however, were determined by two different things which Marx assumed to be given, in a given capitalist economy, at a given point in time. On the one hand, they depended on the existing conditions of production, *both technical and social*, which defined the relations between inputs and outputs in the productive process. On the other hand, they depended on the division of the net product between workers and capitalists in that society. We shall turn to the value quantity representation of the economy below but, for reasons which will emerge later, we start by describing the economy in physical terms.

Consider a very simple economy with three industries. One industry produces the means of production, to be called iron, one produces gold and the third produces a necessary consumption good, say corn. In each industry the production process uses only labour and iron as inputs; the amount of iron used per unit of labour varies between the industries but, whichever industry iron is used in, it is completely used up in one year. Thus there is no *fixed* capital.

Table I shows the physical inputs to, and physical outputs from each industry, with inputs to the left of the arrows and outputs to the right. (The argument does not, of course, depend on the particular figures given here.) The final row shows the physical inputs and outputs for the economy as a whole.

Table I

	Iron	Labour		Iron	Gold	Corn
Iron industry	28	56	→	56	—	—
Gold industry	16	16	→	—	48	—
Corn industry	12	8	→	—	—	8
Total	56	80	→	56	48	8

Thus the first row shows that 56 units of labour, working with 28 units of iron, produce 56 units of iron; the second shows that 16 units of labour, working with 16 units of iron, produce 48 units of gold; while the third shows that eight units of labour, working with 12 units of iron, produce eight units of corn. (The physical units to which we refer might, for example, be thousands of tons in the case of iron and of corn and kilograms in the case of gold. Labour is naturally measured in time-units: for example, thousands of hours. The second row would then state that 16 thousand hours of labour, working with 16 thousand tons of iron, produce 48 kilograms of gold.) The final row, being merely the sum of the first three rows, shows that, in the economy as a whole, 80 units of labour are being performed[2] and 56 units of iron are being used up, while 56 units of iron, 48 units of gold and eight units of corn are being produced. Since the output of iron = 56 units = the amount of iron used up in production, it will be clear that our economy cannot expand (this is *not* important for the questions we wish to examine). *Net* output therefore consists of 48 units of gold and eight units of corn. We shall assume that the total real wage bill paid to the 80 units of labour consists of five units of corn, this corn wage bill being paid at the beginning of the year, as assumed by Marx. The capitalists receive, at the end of each year, 48 units of gold and three units of corn.[3]

(Thus, of the eight units of corn available at the end of a year, three units go to the capitalists as part of their profit for that year, while five go to the workers as wages for the *next* year.)

Value and surplus value

By the value of a commodity, Marx meant the quantity of labour

[2] In summing the various labour-times performed in the three different industries, one *evidently* treats these labour-times as equal, ignoring the different, concrete activities which they perform.

[3] It goes without saying that the total output of iron remains in the hands of the capitalists, being first held exclusively by the iron industry capitalists and then being distributed, through the market, between all three sets of capitalists.

socially necessary for the production of that commodity.[4] This value, or quantity of labour, includes, of course, not only the labour used directly in the production of the commodity but also the labour used indirectly in its production or, in other words, the labour required to produce the means of production used up in the direct labour process. Let the values of a unit of iron, a unit of gold and a unit of corn be denoted by l_i, l_g and l_c, respectively.

To determine l_i, consider the first row of Table I. The total value of output in the iron industry is clearly $56l_i$. This is made up of 56 units of direct labour-time *plus* the labour embodied in the 28 units of iron used up in production; the latter is simply $28l_i$. Hence $28l_i + 56 = 56l_i$ or

$$l_i = 2.$$

Now that l_i has been determined, l_g and l_c can be found directly. From the second row of Table I we see that $48l_g$ is equal to 16 (direct labour) *plus* the labour embodied in 16 units of iron, the latter simply being $16l_i = 32$. Hence

$$48l_g = 16 + 32 = 48$$

or

$$l_g = 1.$$

In the same way, from the third row of Table I,

$$8l_c = 8 + 12l_i$$

and thus

$$8l_c = 8 + 24 = 32$$

or

$$l_c = 4.$$

It will be noted that the values of the commodities ($l_i = 2$, $l_g = 1$, $l_c = 4$) have been determined solely from the physical data given in Table I; they are quite independent of wages, profits and prices.

While the physical data of Table I are sufficient to determine the

---

[4] *Cf.*, chapter 1 and the Appendix to the present work.

values of iron, gold and corn, however, they do not suffice to determine the value of the commodity *labour power*. The value of labour power is, by definition, the value of the commodities required to maintain the working class, i.e. the commodities necessary to reproduce labour power. The value of labour power, therefore, depends on what quantities of commodities are obtained by the workers, as well as being dependent on the values of these latter commodities. In our example, since labour power is reproduced by the working class's consumption of 5 units of corn, the value of labour power, V, is given by

$$V = 5l_c = 5 \times 4 = 20.$$

Total surplus value, S, follows immediately since $(V+S) =$ total live labour $= 80$; thus

$$S = 80 - V = 80 - 20 = 60.^5$$

It should be noted that, given the total of living labour and the real wage paid, V and S depend only on l_c and that l_c, in turn, depends only on the production conditions in the iron and corn industries. Changes in the production conditions in the gold industry, that is, would have no effect on V or S. (This illustrates the point, often made by Marx, that increases in labour productivity in industries that are not involved, directly or indirectly, in the production of commodities consumed by the workers do not generate 'increases in relative surplus value'.[6] It should also be noted, more generally, that by considering various possible changes in the physical data one can explain, simply and clearly, Marx's concepts of both absolute and relative surplus value.)[7]

Hence from knowledge of the physical conditions of production and the real wage, one can determine values, the value of labour

---

[5] That the calculation is correct may be checked as follows. The capitalists obtain 48 units of gold plus 3 units of corn and the value of these commodities $= 48l_g + 3l_c = 48 \times 1 + 3 \times 4 = 48 + 12 = 60 = S$.

[6] *Cf.*, *Capital*, vol. I, Penguin/NLR, 1976, p. 432.

[7] *Cf.*, chapter 6.

power and surplus value. The *rate* of surplus value, S/V, is then also known (and equal to 60/20 = 300 per cent in our example). From the physical data, that is, one can deduce the value description of the economy, showing how workers are exploited by working part of the time (3/4 in our example) for the capitalists. Indeed we can easily convert Table I into Table II which is the value schema, for our example, as used by Marx. Each entry in the first column of Table I is multiplied by the value of iron ($= l_i = 2$) to give C, each entry in the second column is divided into V and S in the proportions $1:3$ and, finally, the outputs are multiplied by $l_i = 2$, $l_g = 1$ and $l_c = 4$ respectively to give the W's.

Table II

	C	V	S	W
Iron industry	56 +	14 +	42 =	112
Gold industry	32 +	4 +	12 =	48
Corn industry	24 +	2 +	6 =	32
Total	112 +	20 +	60 =	192

It may perhaps be objected, at this point, that we appear to have spent much effort merely to arrive at the point reached by Marx 110 years ago! While it may be of some interest to show how the value schema can be derived from physical quantities, is it important to do so? it may be asked. One answer to this, and not a trivial one, is that it is always worthwhile to analyse concepts into underlying concepts. Physical conditions of production and real wages are subject to different forces and trends of change, so that it is much better to study them separately, even if one's final objective is to study changes in, say, V or S.

The transformation of value and surplus value

We wish to concentrate, however, on another reason for basing the analysis of fundamental relations in political economy on the physical data of production and real wages. This is the fact that, in general, it is not possible to explain the rate of profit and production prices solely on the basis of the data set out in a value schema such as that of Table II.[8] As is well-known, Marx, starting from such a schema, attempted to explain profits and prices in the following way. He asserted that the ratio of *total* surplus value to *total* constant and variable capital determined the rate of profit. He then determined a 'price of production' for each commodity by multiplying the appropriate $(C + V)$ by $(1 + \text{the rate of profit})$. Applying this procedure to our example, Marx would have obtained the following results:

$$\text{Rate of profit} = \frac{60}{112+20} = \tfrac{5}{11} = 45\tfrac{5}{11}\%$$

$$\text{Iron price of production} = (56+14) \times (1+\tfrac{5}{11}) = 101\tfrac{9}{11}$$

$$\text{Gold price of production} = (32+4) \times (1+\tfrac{5}{11}) = 52\tfrac{4}{11}$$

$$\text{Corn price of production} = (24+2) \times (1+\tfrac{5}{11}) = 37\tfrac{9}{11}$$

On the basis of his argument Marx 'showed', and this is naturally confirmed by our example, that the aggregate price of production equals the aggregate value and that total profit equals total surplus value.

Now Marx's argument cannot be regarded as acceptable. We may note first that while Marx transformed the values of outputs into prices of production he did not so transform either the value of iron used as input (the C terms are unchanged), or the value of corn advanced as wages (the V terms are unchanged). Thus both iron and corn appear to have different exchange values when sold as output from when they are purchased as inputs; but this is nonsensical since

[8] See chapter 4 for a more detailed discussion.

sale and purchase are two aspects of the same transaction. Hence inputs must be transformed as well as outputs. (Marx knew this and drew attention to it but does not appear ever to have modified his calculations accordingly.)

Merely allowing for the transformation of the inputs will not, however, suffice to produce a coherent theory of profits and prices.[9] The more fundamental flaw in Marx's argument lies at the beginning of it, when he equates the profit rate to $S/(C + V)$ for the economy as a whole. As Marx himself emphasized, the rate of profit is a concept used in analysing a capitalist economy at the 'level of prices', not at the 'level of values', and the tendency to the uniformity of profit rates as between industries is enforced by the mobility of money capital. Thus the rate of profit is equal to the *price* of gross output minus the *price* of the inputs, divided by the *price* of those inputs. Now, when prices are not proportional to values, there is no reason at all why this ratio should equal the *value* of gross output minus the the *value* of inputs, divided by the *value* of these inputs. (As will be seen below, the two ratios are very different in our economy.) In other words, $S/(C + V)$ is *not* the rate of profit in a capitalist economy.

If we are to explain profits and prices adequately we must leave

---

[9] To see this, let k_i be the price/value ratio for iron and k_c be that for corn and suppose that the profit rate is $(5/11)$ as argued by Marx. If we now transform both inputs and outputs we obtain, from the first and third rows of Table II,

$$(56k_i + 14k_c)\left(1 + \frac{5}{11}\right) = 112k_i$$

and

$$(24k_i + 2k_c)\left(1 + \frac{5}{11}\right) = 32k_c$$

These two relations simplify to

and

$$2k_c = 3k_i$$

$$5k_c = 6k_i$$

respectively. Now the latter equations are simply inconsistent with positive prices; *there are no* positive price/value ratios, k_i and k_c, which satisfy both these relations. Hence the assertion in the text that the problem in Marx's approach lies deeper than his not having transformed input prices.

the value schema and return to the physical quantities description of the economy. *This* is why we started with the latter. In the next section we show how the physical data suffice to determine profits and prices even though the data of the usual value schema do not (in general).

The rate of profit and prices
Following Marx, we shall treat gold as the money commodity, so that the price of a commodity is the quantity of gold with which it exchanges.[10]

Denote the rate of profit by r and let w, p_i and p_c be the money wage rate per unit of labour-time, the money price per unit of iron and the money price per unit of corn respectively. (The money price of a unit of gold is, of course, unity by definition.) Now consider, together, the first row of Table I and the following equation:

$$(1 + r)(28p_i + 56w) = 56p_i.$$

This equation says that the price of the iron and labour inputs in the iron industry, multiplied by one plus the profit rate, equals the price of the iron industry output. The latter price, that is, covers the price of the capital advanced *plus* profits at the rate r on that capital.

In the same manner we have, for the gold and corn industries respectively,

$$(1 + r)(16p_i + 16w) = 48$$

and

$$(1 + r)(12p_i + 8w) = 8p_c.$$

Furthermore, since the money wages paid to the workers must just

[10] Since one unit of gold is produced by one unit of labour ($l_g = 1$), it follows that the price of a commodity is numerically equal to the labour embodied in the gold with which that commodity exchanges. This can be compared with the value of that commodity.

enable them to purchase five units of corn, it must be true that

$$80w = 5p_c.$$

There are thus four equations to determine the four variables r, w, p_i, p_c. The (approximate) solutions are[11]

$$r = 52.08\%, \; w = 0.2685$$

$$p_i = 1.7052, \; p_c = 4.2960$$

It will be noted at once that the rate of profit, 52.08 per cent, is very different from that given by Marx's formula $S/(C+V)$, i.e. $45\frac{5}{11}$ per cent. In other words, $S/(C+V)$ does not even give a good approximation to the profit rate.

Some rather tedious calculations show that the aggregate price of output (approximately 178) is *not* equal to the aggregate value of output (192) and that total profit (approximately 61) is *not* equal to total surplus value (60). (Nor does either of the elements of capital have an aggregate price equal to aggregate value.) The idea that total profit equals total surplus value is just as false as the idea that $S/(C+V)$ is the rate of profit.

It is not difficult to see that the second of our four equations, that relating to gold production, is relevant to the determination of w, p_i and p_c (which are all money quantities) but is irrelevant to the determination of r.[12] Other things being equal, a change in the

---

[11] It may be of interest to note that in the limiting case of workers obtaining the whole net product (8 units of corn and 48 units of gold), the equation $80w = 5p_c$ would have to be replaced by $80w = (8p_c + 48)$; the solution would then be

$$r = \text{zero}, w = 1$$
$$p_i = 2 = l_i, \; p_c = 4 = l_c.$$

[12] To see this, ignore the second of our four equations and divide through each of the others by p_c. There are then three equations and only three unknowns, namely r and the *ratios* (w/p_c) and (p_i/p_c). Thus r can be determined, as can (w/p_c) and (p_i/p_c), quite independently of production conditions in the gold industry. The latter conditions merely determine, via the second equation, the absolute levels of w, p_i and p_c. The point being made here has been emphasized by Paul Sweezy (following Bortkiewicz) in ch. 7 of his *Theory of Capitalist Development*, London, 1962; see, in particular, pp. 123–5.

production conditions for gold will have no effect on the profit rate. This gives another way of seeing that $S/(C+V)$ is not the rate of profit; for while S and V depend only on the real corn wage and on the production conditions for iron and corn, total C depends on the production conditions for gold as well. Thus if the latter change, while all other physical conditions remain the same, $S/(C+V)$ will change but the profit rate, r, will not; clearly, then, the former can equal the latter only by a fluke.

A warning about gold money

In the discussion above, we have deliberately followed Marx in treating money as a produced commodity, gold, in order to facilitate comparison between his analysis and ours. It is most important to remember, however, that money today consists, essentially, not of gold but of pieces of paper and, even more important, of mere numbers written in books or stored in computer memories (bank deposits). While gold is still used in the settlement of some international payments, it is effectively irrelevant *within* modern capitalist economies. It is therefore not possible to base the analysis of modern monetary questions, e.g. inflation, on theories of value and price which assume a commodity money such as gold. The above analysis would, therefore, be more appropriate to contemporary problems if one struck out the gold industry. This, as has been explained above,[13] would have no effect on the determination of r and would still leave determinate the *ratios* (w/p_i), (w/p_c) and (p_i/p_c). It would, however, leave for further analysis the determination of absolute money wages and prices.

Principal conclusions

Starting from the physical conditions of production and the real wage, one can derive values and surplus value, showing how the values of commodities other than labour power depend only on the

---

[13] See the preceding footnote 12.

(technically *and socially* determined) physical conditions of production, while the value of labour power and surplus value depend, in addition, on the real wages of the workers. The nature of exploitation is thus revealed, as is the fact that V and S are independent of the conditions in industries irrelevant to the production of wage goods. One can also derive from the physical picture of the economy a coherent theory of profits and prices. In doing so, however, one finds that, in general,[14] profits and prices *cannot* be derived from the ordinary value schema, that $S/(C+V)$ is *not* the rate of profit and that total profit is *not* equal to total surplus value. Thus not only can one build the theory of profits and prices around the physical schema, rather than the value schema, but one is forced to do so.

It may be helpful to represent our principal conclusions as in Figure I.

Figure I

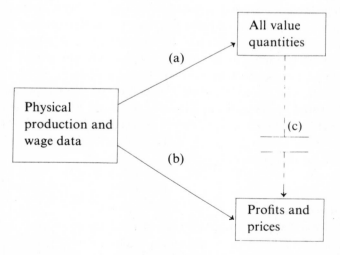

[14] In order to make the numerical example as simple as possible, we have assumed only one produced means of production (iron) and only one wage

The solid arrow labelled (a) shows that from the physical data all the value quantities may be explained (in our example, l_i, l_g, l_c, V, S and the value schema set out in Table II). Arrow (b) shows that from the same data one can explain profits and prices, etc. (in our example, r, w, p_i, p_c, total profit, etc.). The dashed and 'blocked off' arrow (c) represents the fact that one cannot, in general, explain profits and prices from value quantities as set out in the usual value schema, that $S/(C + V)$ is not the rate of profit, etc.

We thus have to picture our theoretical structure as having a 'fork-like' character, with a 'value prong', arrow (a), and a 'profit-price prong', arrow (b). *There is*, in general, *no way from one prong to the other*. This conclusion, it should perhaps be emphasized, is the conclusion of an argument in logic; should anyone wish to challenge it, they must do so either by finding a logical flaw in the argument[15] or by rejecting explicitly and coherently one or more of the assumptions on which it is based. They cannot challenge this conclusion by, for example, merely remarking that it differs from Marx's conclusion or by asserting, whether rightly or wrongly, that the conclusion is politically or ideologically 'unacceptable'.

---

good (corn). This has the disadvantage that one *can* therefore derive profits and prices from Table II, *in this example*, (provided, of course, that one follows the method of Bortkiewicz and not that of Marx). The need for simplicity has thus meant that the example does not *fully* illustrate the general truths asserted here. That they are general truths will, however, be seen in the next chapter.

[15] *Nota bene:* the present type of argument has been examined, in various forms, by many different writers over the last 80 years. The same conclusions have always been reached and no logical flaw has ever been found in such arguments.

4

Value, Price and Profit
Further Considered

While the simple numerical example of chapter 3 should have
sufficed to alert attention both to a number of defects in Marx's
arguments and to a possible way of overcoming them, numerical
examples always arouse in the reader's mind the legitimate question
whether the conclusions reached are really of general validity.[1] It will
therefore be shown in this chapter that the general conclusions
reached in the preceding one do indeed hold good in any capitalist
economy with no fixed capital, no joint products, a uniform wage
rate and a uniform rate of profit. All the background assumptions
set out in chapter 1 are, of course, to be taken as read.

The determination of the rate of profit
Consider then a simple capitalist economy in which the known
methods of production comprise only one possible (single product)
method for the production of each of n commodities. Let the gross
output of each commodity be unity by a suitable choice of units, let
the matrix of produced means of production be A, where the jth
column of A shows the inputs used up in industry j, and let a be the
row vector showing the level of employment in each industry. The sum
of the elements of a, i.e. total employment, will be denoted by L. If

---

[1] Except, of course, when a numerical example is used as a *counter-example*
to an allegedly general proposition: a single example is perfectly adequate in
such a context.

the rate of profit over the common period of production is r, if the row vector of money prices is p^m and if the money wage rate, m, is paid in advance, then

$$(1+r)(p^m A + ma) = p^m. \tag{1}$$

In words, the gross money revenue in industry j, p_j^m, is equal to the total money capital advanced in that industry, both for produced means of production and as wages, *plus* profits on that total capital at the uniform rate r. Relation (1) may now be rewritten as

or

$$p^m[I - (1+r)A] = (1+r)ma$$
$$p^m = m(1+r)a[I - (1+r)A]^{-1}, \tag{2}$$

provided only that production conditions permit the production of net output and that the rate of profit, r, is less than the maximum possible rate of profit (i.e., that real wages are positive).[2]

Relation (2) does not, of course, determine either r or p^m; it simply shows how they are related to one another. Now, however, let the real wage bundle obtained by the workers be given by the (non-zero) column vector w. Given that workers do not save, their money wages just enable them to purchase the real wage at the ruling money prices. Hence

$$mL = p^m \cdot w \tag{3}$$

Thus on post-multiplying both sides of (2) by w, and taking account of (3), one obtains, after dividing through by m,

$$L = (1+r)a[I - (1+r)A]^{-1}w. \tag{4}$$

In (4), L, a, A and w are all known: the only unknown is r. The right-hand side of (4) is known to be a monotonically increasing function of r, tending to infinity as r approaches the maximum rate

---

[2] See, for example, G. Debreu and I. N. Herstein, 'Non-Negative Square Matrices', *Econometrica*, 1953; R. M. Solow, 'On the Structure of Linear Models', *ibid.*, 1952.

of profit.[3] Thus, subject to the one condition $L > a(I-A)^{-1}w$, to be discussed below, relation (4) determines a unique, positive value of r. The rate of profit is determined by the physical conditions of production, expressed by A, a and L, and by the workers' real wages, w. (The prices p^m are now also determined, through (2), in terms of the same data, for any given *money* wage rate, m.)

It will not have escaped the reader's notice that the above determination of the rate of profit, in terms of physical production conditions and real wages, involved no reference to *any* concept of embodied labour-time. Even if it were possible to determine the rate of profit (and prices of production) in terms of labour-time values, aggregate S, C and V, etc., such a determination would be redundant. Production conditions and real wages, which Marx himself often treated as data, are sufficient for the determination of the profit rate.

Once the above point has been firmly grasped, it becomes clear that *there is no problem of transforming values into prices*, etc., *to be solved*. The 'transformation problem' is a 'non-problem', a spurious problem which can only be thought to arise and to have significance when one is under the misapprehension that the rate of profit must be determined in terms of labour quantities. Once it is seen that there is no such necessity, the 'problem' simply evaporates.

Aliter

The above determination of the rate of profit may also be presented in an alternative form. If relation (3) is used to eliminate m from (1), one obtains

$$(1+r)p^m(A+L^{-1}w \cdot a) = p^m. \tag{5}[4]$$

Now since p^m must be a strictly positive vector, it follows from (5)

---

[3] See, again, Debreu and Herstein, *op. cit.* and Solow, *op. cit.*, referred to in footnote 2.

[4] It should be noted that since w is a *column* vector and a is a *row* vector, $w \cdot a$ is an $n \times n$ *matrix*, which is not to be confused with the scalar $a \cdot w$.

that $(1+r)^{-1}$ must be the Perron–Frobenius root[5] of $(A+L^{-1}w \cdot a)$. Thus, in an obvious notation to be used throughout this work,

$$(1+r)^{-1} = \lambda^{PF}(A+L^{-1}w \cdot a). \tag{6}$$

Relation (6) presents, perhaps even more clearly than does (4), the determination of the profit rate, r, in terms of the conditions of production – A, L, a – and real wages, w. Again, no reference to *any* concept of embodied labour-time is involved.

It will be clear from (6) that the rate of profit, r, can be positive only if

$$\lambda^{PF}(A+L^{-1}w \cdot a) < 1. \tag{7}$$

Inequality (7) thus provides the condition which must be satisfied by the methods of production and real wages if the economic system in question is to be productive from the capitalist standpoint, i.e. to generate profits. [It is to be noted that that same inequality is the condition which must be satisfied if i) the system is to be capable of producing a physical net product for capitalists (*net* of wages that is) and ii) the system is to be capable of 'producing surplus labour' (employing an amount of labour greater than required in producing the real wages for that amount of labour, together with the means of production used for that purpose). The conditions for profitability, production of physical surplus and 'production' of surplus labour are thus identical.]

Further remarks
Of the n commodities produced, only some will enter the wage bundle w, i.e. many elements of w will be zero. Of those which do not enter the wage bundle, some will nevertheless be used, directly or indirectly, in producing one or more commodities consumed by workers; while the remaining commodities will neither be wage goods nor be used at any stage in the production of wage goods. The

---

[5] See the appendix to the present chapter for the meaning of this term.

important division, for present purposes, is that between commodities which are wage goods and/or are used in producing wage goods, on the one hand and, on the other, those commodities which are not wage goods and are not used, either directly or indirectly, in the production of such goods. Let the first set of commodities be commodities, 1, 2, . . ., h and the second set therefore be commodities $h+1, h+2, \ldots, n$.

Denote the complete matrix on the left-hand side of (5) by A^+. It may now be partitioned as

$$A^+ \equiv \begin{bmatrix} A_1^+ & A_2^+ \\ 0 & A_4^+ \end{bmatrix},$$

where A_1^+ is an $h \times h$ matrix and A_4^+ is an $(n-h) \times (n-h)$ matrix. The sub-matrix A_3^+ *must* be zero, for otherwise at least one of commodities $h+1, \ldots, n$ would either enter the wage bundle or be used as a direct input into at least one of industries $1, \ldots, h$, contrary to hypothesis. If p^m is now partitioned correspondingly, into p^h and p^n, say, (5) can be written as

$$(1+r)p^h A_1^+ = p^h \tag{8}$$

$$(1+r)[p^h A_2^+ + p^n A_4^+] = p^n. \tag{9}$$

Reasoning as before, it follows from (8) that[6]

$$(1+r)^{-1} = \lambda^{PF}(A_1^+). \tag{10}$$

The rate of profit depends only on the elements of A_1^+, that is, on the *positive* elements of the wage bundle and the (direct and indirect) production conditions of those wage goods. The production conditions for commodities $h+1, \ldots, n$ have *no* influence on the rate of profit. Nor do they influence p^h, the production prices of the first h

---

[6] Provided, that is, that $\lambda^{PF}(A_1^+) > \lambda^{PF}(A_4^+)$. This is an acceptable condition, however, for were it not satisfied, the solution to (8) would be $p^h = O$, hardly an economically significant situation. Note that, as long as this condition is satisfied, (6) and (10) are entirely consistent; $\lambda^{PF}(A^+) = \lambda^{PF}(A_1^+)$.

commodities; they affect only the prices of commodities $h+1$, ..., n.

Either (4) or (10) may be used to show that, other things being equal, the rate of profit is a decreasing function of every element of the real wage bundle. Thus suppose that A_1^+, in (10), is irreducible;[7] $\lambda^{PF}(A_1^+)$ is then an increasing function of each of its elements and, therefore, of each element of the real wage bundle. Consequently, r is a *decreasing* function of every such element, since $(1+r)^{-1} = \lambda^{PF}(A_1^+)$. Alternatively, it may be noted that the right-hand side of (4) is an increasing function not only of r but also of every element of w; it follows immediately that, other things equal, a change in any element of w will lead to a change of the opposite sign in r. Relations such as (4) and (10) may also be used to show how, for given w, r will vary with changes in hours of work, speed-up, etc.: these questions will be considered in chapter 6.

Values and the rate of surplus value

The amount of labour 'embodied' in each commodity, total surplus value, the rate of surplus value, etc. can be deduced at once from the data, A, a, L and w.

Let the row vector l show the values of – the total, socially necessary labour-times embodied in – the various commodities. Since the gross output of each commodity is unity, Marx's 'value accounts', stating that the value of each commodity j is equal to $(c_j + v_j + s_j)$, can be written as

$$lA + a = l, \tag{11}$$

where lA is the row vector of 'c' quantities and a is the row vector of 'v + s' quantities. Thus

$$l = a(I - A)^{-1}. \tag{12}$$

The values of commodities depend only on their conditions of production, being independent, in particular, of w and of r.

[7] See, again, the works cited in footnote 2 and the appendix to this chapter.

The aggregate value of labour-power, V, however, depends both on l and on w.[8] In fact

$$V = l \cdot w \qquad (13)$$

or

$$V = a(I - A)^{-1}w, \qquad (14)$$

from (12). V depends both on real wages and on their conditions of production; note that, by an extension of the argument given in the previous section, V does not depend on the production conditions of commodities $h + 1, \ldots, n$ – as Marx frequently and correctly pointed out. Total surplus value, S, is given by

$$S = L - V \qquad (15)$$

or

$$S = [L - a(I - A)^{-1}w],$$

from (14). Total S depends only on the total labour done, on the real wage and on the conditions of its production; it is independent of the production conditions of commodities $h + 1, \ldots, n$. The total value of constant capital, C, is of course equal to the *sum* of the elements of lA.

Thus l, V, S and C can be determined in terms of the conditions of production and the real wage. Indeed, they cannot be determined in any other way. The 'quantity of labour-time socially necessary for the production of a given commodity' has no meaning except with reference to the physical conditions of production. Again, 'the labour-time required to produce the means of subsistence' has no meaning except with reference to the real, physically specified wage bundle and to the conditions of its production. Not only can Marx's magnitudes l, V, S and C be derived from the physical conditions of

[8] *Cf.*, vol. I, *op. cit.*, p. 276: 'The value of labour-power can be resolved into the value of a definite quantity of the means of subsistence. It therefore varies with the value of the means of subsistence, i.e. with the quantity of labour-time required to produce them.'

production and the real wage but they *must* be; there is no other meaningful basis for their determination. There is, of course, no reason to think that Marx would have disputed this; on the contrary, much that he wrote can sensibly be interpreted to mean that he regarded l, V, S and C as the most appropriate indices of the technical and social conditions of production and of real wages. The point is nonetheless important, for since Marx's various labour-time magnitudes are entirely *derivative* of the physically specified real wages and production conditions, these latter physical quantities being fully adequate to the determination of the profit rate and the prices of production, it follows at once that the labour-time magnitudes are of no significance for that determination.

Exploitation and profits

It was stated above that (4) determines a unique, positive rate of profit, subject to the one condition that

$$L > a(I - A)^{-1} w.$$

It may now be seen, from (14) and (15), that this condition may be written as

$$V + S > V$$

or

$$S > 0. \qquad (16)$$

The rate of profit will be positive if and only if surplus labour (surplus value) is positive.

It is to be noted carefully i) that this proposition is rather obvious and ii) that it does not, in itself, constitute a theory of the existence of profits:

i) The rate of profit is positive only if the total money value of profits is positive and that can be so only if capitalists appropriate a positive quantity of at least one commodity. Since a positive quantity of labour is required, directly or indirectly, for the production of every commodity, the rate of profit is thus positive only if some labour is done which is *not* directed towards the direct or indirect production of the wage bundle; i.e. only if surplus labour is performed. Conversely, if surplus labour is performed, the capitalists appropriate a positive quantity of least one commodity, therefore money profits are positive and therefore the rate of profit is positive. That r is positive if and only if S is positive is, in the present context,[9] true but rather obvious.

ii) The very fact that the proposition in question 'runs both ways' (r is positive *if and only if* S is positive) means at once that it does not constitute a theory of why r is positive. Any theory of *why profits are positive* will at the same time, be a theory of why surplus value is positive. Neo-classical economists do not commonly invoke the concept of surplus labour but they could do so without causing the slightest inconsistency within their theory.[10] A vulgar neo-classical economist might then say, 'The capital-labour ratio is finite; therefore the marginal product of capital is positive; therefore the rate of profit is positive; therefore surplus labour is positive'. Again, a more sophisticated neo-classical might say, 'Time preference is positive; therefore the rate of profit is positive; therefore surplus labour is positive'. Whatever the demerits of these (and other) neo-classical theories – none of which is advocated here – these imaginary statements suffice to show that asserting the co-existence of profits and surplus labour does not, *in itself,* provide a theory of why profits are positive.

Thus the only possible role, in a theory of profits, for the statement

[9] The argument is not so simple in the context of fixed capital and pure joint products. See chapters 10, 11, 12 and 13.

[10] Any reader inclined to an immediate, emotional rejection of this statement, should pause for reflection – and re-read paragraph i) above. Böhm-Bawerk, one of Marx's most significant neo-classical critics, did *not* seek to deny the existence of surplus labour but sought rather to show that it existed *because of* 'time preference' and the 'productivity of roundabout production'. Whatever may be the answer to the question, 'Why do neo-classical economists not refer to surplus labour?' the fact is that they could do so, without abandoning their existing theories.

that 'r is positive if and only if S is positive' is as the final link in an argument, the earlier stages of which show *why S is positive*. This point is not intended to appear original or striking; it is taken for granted by many Marxist writers. It does, nevertheless, carry a significant implication. A Marxist theory of profits must be directed to explaining *why* the social, political and technical conditions in a capitalist society are such that the condition

$$L > a(I - A)^{-1}w$$

is permanently satisfied. Now such an explanation must necessarily run in terms of the *determinants* of the conditions of production and real wages. Marx's value magnitudes, however, far from being determinants of those factors are precisely derivative from them; consequently they can play *no essential* role in the theory of why profits are positive. The essential elements of such a theory may well include the classical 'double freedom' of the worker, the analysis of the labour process, the effects of accumulation on employment and real wages, the role of the state, the role of workers' organizations and many other factors discussed by Marx (and later Marxists) but they will *not* include any embodied labour-time magnitudes.

The above point is sufficiently important to merit repetition, in a different formulation. It was seen above that the conditions for positive profits may be written as

$$\lambda^{PF}(A_1^+) = \lambda^{PF}(A + L^{-1}w \cdot a) < 1. \qquad (7), (10)$$

The task is, then, to explain *why* A, L, *a* and *w* are such that conditions (7) and (10) are satisfied and continue to be satisfied. The required explanation is doubtless complex, bringing in many considerations perfectly at home in the general context of a materialist theory of history. Yet one thing is certain – that explanation will have to focus on the *determinants* of A, L, *a* and *w*, which most certainly do not include the merely derivative value magnitudes.

Marx's formulation of the question

After seeing how the rate of profit (and prices of production) can be determined quite independently of (derivative) value magnitudes, it may be of interest to consider Marx's method of argument.

No explicit reference was made above to the precise nature of the money in which wages and prices were measured, for the simple reason that the conclusions reached were independent of that precise nature. Suppose now, as Marx did throughout much (though not all) of his writing, that money is the produced commodity gold, so that p^m and m are now gold money prices and wages respectively. Relation (2), reproduced here for convenience, still holds good.

$$p^m = m(1+r)a[I - (1+r)A]^{-1}. \tag{2}$$

Now, however, there is an additional equation involved: the gold price of one unit of gold is necessarily unity. Thus if $m_j(r)$ is the jth column of the matrix on the right of (2) and if commodity g is gold,[11] then

$$p_g^m = 1 = m(1+r)a \cdot m_g(r). \tag{17}$$

Since r is still determined by (4) above, (17) determines the gold wage rate, m. Dividing through (2) by (17), one sees that the gold price of commodity j is given by

$$p_j^m = \left[\frac{a \cdot m_j(r)}{a \cdot m_g(r)}\right], \tag{18}$$

where r is determined by (4). This is what Marx calls the price of commodity j.

If w were such that r were zero, then (18) would, of course, become

$$p_j^m = \left[\frac{a \cdot m_j(o)}{a \cdot m_g(o)}\right]$$

or

$$p_j^m = (l_j/l_g). \tag{19}$$

[11] No reference is made here to the previous division of commodities into the first h and the last (n − h) commodities.

This was what Marx often called 'the value' of commodity j, on the grounds that, while l_j is the basic meaning of 'the value of j', that value is socially 'expressed' or 'represented' by an amount of gold with the same 'value' when commodities exchange in proportion to their values.[12] Thus when Marx asserted that total profit equals total surplus value (or that total price equals total value), he was asserting that

$$\Sigma_{j=1}^n \left[\frac{a \cdot m_j(r)}{a \cdot m_g(r)}\right] x_j = \Sigma_{j=1}^n (l_j/l_g) x_j,$$

where the x_j are the physical quantities of commodities appropriated by the capitalists (or the total quantities produced). In either case the assertion was, in effect, that gold is an 'average commodity', so that while, when r is positive, $p_j^m > (l_j/l_g)$ for some commodities, $p_j^m < (l_j/l_g)$ holds for others, with the differences 'cancelling out' in aggregate.[13] It is self-evident that such a 'cancellation' can occur only by a fluke, for a given aggregate of commodities at a given r; change the x_j and/or the value of r and the 'price' and 'value' aggregates will diverge. Simultaneous 'cancellation' for *two different* aggregates would be even more of a fluke. (The simple counter-example of the previous chapter shows that neither of Marx's assertions need hold.)

That total profit and total surplus value are, in general, different might be thought to leave open the possibility that Marx's formula for the rate of profit, $(S/C+V)$, is still correct. Yet it has already been shown, implicitly, that this is not so. The rate of profit, r, total V and total S depend only on L, w and the production conditions of w. Total C, however, depends *in addition* on the production conditions of commodities $(h+1), \ldots, n$. Thus if the latter had been different, whilst everything else had been the same, C, and consequently $(S/C + V)$, would have been different but the rate of profit, r, would not. Thus r and $(S/C+V)$ *cannot*, in general, be equal.[14]

[12] See the Appendix to this work.
[13] *Cf.* Marx's discussion of Ricardo's treatment of gold as an 'average commodity' in *Theories of Surplus Value*, Part II, London, 1969, p. 199.
[14] The condition for their (fluke) equality will be considered in chapter 12.

62

A spurious impression

Let (5) be rewritten as

$$(1+r)p\mathbf{A}^+ = p, \qquad (5')$$

where the notation $\mathbf{A}^+ \equiv (\mathbf{A} + \mathbf{L}^{-1}w \cdot a)$ has been adopted and the superscripts have been dropped from the price vectors, since $(5')$ is clearly independent of the standard in which prices are measured. If $\hat{l}$ is the diagonal matrix of labour values, $(5')$ can be modified to

$$(1+r)(p \cdot \hat{l}^{-1})(\hat{l}\mathbf{A}^+\hat{l}^{-1}) = (p \cdot \hat{l}^{-1}). \qquad (20)$$

Now $(p \cdot \hat{l}^{-1})$ is a row vector of prices relative to labour values, while $(\hat{l}\mathbf{A}^+\hat{l}^{-1})$ is an $n \times n$ matrix in which the jth column shows the *values* of the n commodity quantities used, both as material inputs and as wage goods, per unit of *value* of gross output. The column *sum* of column j is thus $(c_j + v_j)$ in the traditional Marxist notation but the individual elements of that column show the separate commodity values which make up $(c_j + v_j)$. Thus $(\hat{l}\mathbf{A}^+\hat{l}^{-1})$ can be thought of as a (disaggregated) $(c+v)$ matrix, while $(p \cdot \hat{l}^{-1})$ can be interpreted as a vector of 'price-value coefficients'. Subject to conditions analogous to those mentioned in the discussion of (10), (20) determines r as

$$(1+r)^{-1} = \lambda^{PF}(\hat{l}\mathbf{A}^+\hat{l}^{-1}). \qquad (21)$$

Now result (21) is perfectly sound but it is important not to be misled by it into thinking that the rate of profit, r, is after all 'determined by value magnitudes', let alone into thinking that $r = S/C + V$. It may be noted first that (10) and (21) do, indeed, determine the same value of r. It may be noted further that the same would be true of

$$(1+r)^{-1} = \lambda^{PF}(\hat{d}\mathbf{A}^+\hat{d}^{-1}),$$

where $\hat{d}$ is any diagonal matrix with all positive elements along the diagonal! This shows at once how superficial is the difference between (10) and (21); when it is remembered, in addition, that l is purely derivative of $\mathbf{A}$, a, it will be seen that relation (21) is in no way a superior alternative to (10) but is merely a pointlessly complicated version of it.

Since (10) and (21) determine the same value of r, it follows that (21) does *not* determine r as equal to $S/C + V$, in general. Finally, it should be noted explicitly that (20) and (21) do *not* justify any attempt to determine the rate of profit and prices of production from the traditional kind of value schema in which, for each industry, all the 'c' elements are added together and all the 'v' elements are added together. Such an attempt would be legitimate only in the exceptional circumstance that all elements of constant capital had the same price-value coefficient *and* all elements of variable capital had the same price-value coefficient; since some commodities enter both constant and variable capital, this in effect requires that *all* commodities have the same price-value coefficient, i.e. that prices are proportional to values and that the whole (non-) problem of transformation is absent.

In brief, it is possible greatly to complicate (5′) by writing it as (20) but nothing whatever is gained by doing this, given that one does not regard as a gain an increased possibility of confusion and misunderstanding. If formulation (20) creates the impression that (5′) is being abandoned and that value magnitudes are essential to the determination of r, then it must be stated clearly that that impression is entirely spurious.[15]

[15] In his paper 'The "Transformation Problem"', (*Review of Economic Studies*, 1956–57), F. Seton presented the determination of the profit rate (and prices of production) in terms of relations such as (20) and (21). Seton cannot be held responsible for any misunderstanding about the relationship between the 'value' determination and the 'physical' determination, however. He expressly stated, in his eighth footnote, that, in our notation, $\lambda^{PF}(A^+) = \lambda^{PF}(\hat{l}A^+\hat{l}^{-1})$. Unfortunately this has not prevented such writers as Gerstein, *op. cit.* and Fine and Harris, *op. cit.*, from 'inventing' a significant difference between the physical and the value determinations, to the effect that the former is more superficial! In fact, as has been seen, the difference is that the value determination is just a clumsy, derivative form of the physical one. (This remark should not be taken as a criticism of Seton's paper; Seton set himself to examine the traditional formulation of the problem and did so with great clarity.)

Choice of technique

It has been assumed above that only one known method is available for the production of each of the n commodities. Now while neo-classical economists often greatly exaggerate the number of alternative production methods available, between which capitalists choose on profit maximizing grounds, the fact remains that there are technique choices to be made by capitalists. Steel can be made with blast furnaces or with electric arc furnaces, power stations can be driven by coal or by oil – or, in some cases, by water-power – and so on. Indeed, the very fact of technical progress ensures that there are technique choices to be made by capitalists.

Faced with one or more available methods for the production of each commodity and with a given real wage bundle which must be paid to each worker, capitalists in each industry will seek to adopt that production method which minimizes costs and maximizes the rate of profit. The forces of competition will lead to that selection of production method, industry by industry, which generates the highest possible uniform rate of profit throughout the economy.

It is not difficult to determine which methods will be used and what the resulting rate of profit (and prices of production) will be.[16] Let there be N_j alternative methods for the production of commodity j. The number of logically possible ways of selecting one process for each industry is then $N \equiv N_1 \times N_2 \times N_3 \times \ldots \times N_n$. Each one of these N combinations, together with the real wage per unit of labour paid in advance, will then define an A^+ matrix. The corresponding rate of profit will, of course, be given by $(1 + r)^{-1} = \lambda^{PF}(A^+)$. That combination of methods will be chosen which generates the highest value of r (and the lowest money price of each commodity relative to the money wage). The choice of methods, the rate of profit and the prices of production will thus have been determined, by a repeated application of the physical quantities theory of r.

What have any value magnitudes to contribute to this analysis?

[16] Constant returns to scale will be assumed in this section and the *absolute* levels of output and of employment will thus be ignored.

Nothing. The labour values of commodities, or of any aggregates of commodities, are known only when it is known which methods of production are in use. The choice of production methods is itself determined, however, only in the process of determining the maximum achievable rate of profit. Values can therefore be known only *after* the rate of profit has already been determined! The determination of the profit rate is thus *logically prior* to any determination of value magnitudes – it is hardly surprising, then, that the latter have nothing to contribute to the former.

When there is a choice of technique, any attempt to ground the theory of the rate of profit on any value magnitudes must be ill-conceived – and there always is some choice of technique.[17]

Conclusion

It has been shown, within the context of a very simple capitalist economy with no fixed capital and no pure joint products, that the rate of profit is fully determined by the real wage and by the available methods of production, as are the prices of production and the choice of which methods are actually used. The rate of profit is not, other than by a fluke, equal to $S/C + V$. More generally, no value magnitude plays any significant role in the determination of the profit rate (or of prices of production). All value quantities are purely derivative of the physical conditions of production and the real wage and, indeed, in the presence of a choice of technique – which does always exist – those value quantities can only be determined *after* the rate of profit has already been determined in the profit maximizing choice of technique.

It has also been shown that, within the present context, the rate of

[17] It may also be noted that if the real wage should just happen to be such that two different combinations of production methods yield the maximum rate of profit, then the choice of methods – and hence the values of commodities – will not be fully determinate, even though the profit rate and the prices of production are fully determined. This again shows the essential unimportance of value magnitudes in determining r. *Cf.*, M. Morishima, *Marx's Economics, op. cit.*, pp. 188–90.

profit is positive if and only if surplus value is positive. It must be noted, however, both that the demonstration of this proposition is entirely independent of any relationship between values and prices of production and that the proposition does not, in itself, constitute a theory of why profits are positive. Such a theory must focus on the determinants of the (technical and social) conditions of production and of the real wage; even if those determinants are wholly contained within the normal framework of a materialist conception of history, they cannot include, in any essential way, any value magnitudes, simply because these latter are derivative of the things to be explained.

There is not, in any significant sense, any 'transformation problem' to be solved. Since value magnitudes are irrelevant to the proximate determination of the profit rate and of production prices, no issue of the relation between values and prices, or of that between profit and surplus value, ever arises. (Indeed such questions are essentially irrelevant even to the demonstration of the proposition that profits are positive if and only if surplus value is positive.)

These various matters must not be clouded by resort to such responses as 'The physically based analysis is merely superficial; the value based theory penetrates beyond mere appearances', or 'The physical analysis is asocial and ahistorical; only a value based theory can bring out the social nature of economic relations, the role of property and power relationships, the significance of the labour process, etc.', or again 'The Sraffa-based arguments are merely pedantic, dealing with secondary issues of small importance; value theory provides a fully adequate interpretation of the major issues at hand'. This last response is perhaps sufficiently vulgar to require no further comment but it is worth noting that the first response is itself a merely superficial *assertion*, repetition of which will not alter the fact that many of Marx's value based propositions are false, that the physical analysis is actually the only possible foundation for value analysis and that the physical analysis, far from being a terminus to enquiry, precisely points to the issues which require further investigation. As to the second kind of response sketched above, it need only be noted that if it *were* true (it is not) that the conditions of production and the real wage are 'asocial and ahistorical' then it would follow that all value magnitudes possessed the very same properties, since they are merely derivates of the physical conditions! (In fact, of course, the conditions of production and the real wage are saturated with their social and historical determinations.)

The Sraffa-based theory of the rate of profit starts, it must be noted, from *objective* data, referring to elements which might be expected to figure centrally (not, of course, exclusively) in any materialist analysis of history. The latter, it need hardly be said, is crucially important *but it does not stand or fall with the analysis of capitalist society based on value magnitudes.* On the contrary, the development of a materialist understanding of the history of capitalist economies is now seriously hampered by the continued attention paid to such theory, with all its flaws and all the attendant confusions which they engender so prolifically. Sweezy's statement[18] that 'If we believe, with Marx and the great classical economists, that profit can be understood only as a deduction from the combined product of social labour, there is no way of dispensing with value calculation and the labour theory of value on which it is based', is quite simply false.

Appendix
Whilst it would be entirely inappropriate to this work to present a full review of all the mathematical concepts employed, it might be helpful to explain *briefly* and *unrigorously* what is meant by the Perron–Frobenius root of a matrix.

The following problem arises in many areas of applied mathematics: given a square matrix, M, is there a scalar λ and a vector x such that

$$Mx = \lambda x? \tag{i}$$

[18] P. M. Sweezy, *Theory of Capitalist Development*, p. 130.

Now if (i) holds then

$$(M - \lambda I)x = 0 \tag{ii}$$

and (ii) has a non-trivial (non-zero) solution for x only if $\det(M - \lambda I)$ = 0. If M is ($n \times n$) then $\det(M - \lambda I) = 0$ is an nth degree poly nomial in λ, with n real and/or complex roots (some of which may be repeated roots). To each solution λ_j, there is a corresponding x satisfying (i); if $M.x_j = \lambda_j x_j$ then $Mk.x_j = \lambda_j k.x_j$, where k is an scalar, so that only the proportions of the elements of x_j are deter mined.

If, now, M is restricted to be an irreducible, non-negative matri. (a matrix, with every element non-negative, such that the rows and columns *cannot* be permuted so that M has a rectangular block o zero elements in its lower left-hand corner), more may be said Specifically; only one of the λ_j will have a strictly positive x_j associ ated with it; that λ_j will be at least as great in modulus as any othe λ_j; that λ_j will be a continuous, increasing function of every elemen of M. If M is square and non-negative but not necessarily irreducible then similar but somewhat weaker results can be established.

The particular λ referred to here is what is called the Perron Frobenius root, λ^{PF}, in the text.

For a *proper* discussion of these matters, the reader may consul such works as those of Debreu and Herstein or of Solow cited in footnote 2 above.

5

An Alternative Presentation – The Dated Labour Analysis

It has been seen in chapters 3 and 4 that, in the context of a simple capitalist economy, with no fixed capital and no pure joint products, the rate of profit (and the associated prices of production) are determined directly by the physical quantities of inputs and outputs and by the real wage bundle obtained by workers. It has been seen, too, that Marx's 'determination' of the profit rate (and prices of production) is invalid. The same results will be examined in this chapter from a slightly different point of view, making use of 'dated labour' analysis (the nature of which will become clear below).[1] It is important to note from the outset that 'dated labour' analysis is an entirely derivative form of analysis and is quite *secondary* to the type of argument presented in chapters 3 and 4. This is both because the dated labour quantities involved can only be obtained by derivation from the primary data concerning physical inputs, outputs and real wages and because dated labour analysis is not applicable at all once fixed capital and pure joint products are allowed for,[2] as they will be, in later chapters, by means of a simple extension of the physical quantities approach.

---

[1] The argument of this chapter draws heavily on the work of P. Garegnani; also relevant is the work of von Bortkiewicz and of V. K. Dmitriev. (For references, see the penultimate footnote to chapter 1, above.) See also P. Sraffa, *Production of Commodities*, chapter VI.

[2] *Cf.*, Sraffa, *op. cit.*, pp. 58–9.

Dated labour analysis

Consider then a simple capitalist economy in which, by a suitable choice of units, one unit of each of n commodities is produced, there being no fixed capital and no pure joint products. The production of the one unit of, say, commodity 1 will have involved the expenditure of a certain amount of labour-time, call it l_{11}, and, of course, the using up of certain specific quantities of the various commodities used as circulating capital. Those specific quantities of commodities will have been produced in the previous period of production and their production will, again, have required the expenditure of a certain amount of labour-time and the using up of certain commodities. This 'second' expenditure of labour-time, to be called l_{12} can be thought of as labour expended *indirectly* on the production of the one unit of commodity 1. The set of commodities used up as l_{12} was expended was, yet again, produced one period earlier requiring the expenditure of l_{13} units of labour-time and the using up of another set of commodities. And so on – at each step the commodities used up may be 'resolved', so to speak, into a yet earlier expenditure of dated labour-time. Thus the production of one unit of commodity 1 is conceived as requiring the expenditure of l_{11} units of labour-time in the 'current' period, l_{12} units one period before, l_{13} units two periods before, and so on for ever, the dated labour quantities l_{1t} tending to zero eventually, as t tends to infinity.[3]

Now let the money wage rate be m and the money price of commodity 1 be p_1^m. Then if wages are paid at the beginning of each (annual) period of production and the annual rate of profit is r, we must have that

$$p_1^m = ml_{11}(1+r) + ml_{12}(1+r)^2 + ml_{13}(1+r)^3 + \ldots \qquad (1$$

The money price of a unit of commodity 1, p_1^m, is equal to the money

[3] The various labour quantities are not defined as the quantities *actually* expended in the historical past but as the quantities which *would have been* expended had technical conditions of production always been just as they are in the 'current' period. The 'resolution' into a backward time series of labour expenditures is thus purely conceptual. See below for an explicit demonstration of this point and of the fact that l_{1t} eventually tends to zero.

wage bill directly incurred in its production, ml_{11}, multiplied by $(1+r)$ since wages are advanced, *plus* the backward chain of money wage bills for the quantities of indirect labour into which the produced means of production have been 'resolved', ml_{12}, ml_{13}, etc., each wage bill being multiplied up by the appropriate factor $(1+r)^t$. It is to be noted explicitly that 'constant capital' is by no means ignored in (1); it is merely presented in a (perhaps) unfamiliar way.

Now let p_1 be the 'labour-commanded' price of commodity 1 – so that, by definition, $p_1 \equiv (p_1^m/m)$ – and rewrite (1) as

$$p_1 = l_{11}(1+r) + l_{12}(1+r)^2 + l_{13}(1+r)^3 + \ldots \qquad (2)$$

It will be clear that an exactly analogous relation holds for each commodity, so that

$$p_2 = l_{21}(1+r) + l_{22}(1+r)^2 + l_{23}(1+r)^3 + \ldots$$

$$\vdots$$

$$p_n = l_{n1}(1+r) + l_{n2}(1+r)^2 + l_{n3}(1+r)^3 + \ldots$$

or, in an obvious vector notation,

$$p = l_1(1+r) + l_2(1+r)^2 + l_3(1+r)^3 + \ldots \qquad (3)$$

Let w be the bundle of commodities going to the workers as real wages. From (3),

$$p \cdot w = (l_1 \cdot w)(1+r) + (l_2 \cdot w)(1+r)^2 + (l_3 \cdot w)(1+r)^3 + \ldots \qquad (4)$$

Now $p \cdot w$ is the 'labour commanded by the real wage bundle', which is necessarily equal to the total amount of labour employed ('live labour'), L say. Thus, defining $L_t \equiv (l_t \cdot w)$, (4) may be written as

$$L = L_1(1+r) + L_2(1+r)^2 + L_3(1+r)^3 + \ldots \qquad (5)$$

As already stated, L and r in (5) are total 'current' employment and the rate of profit, respectively. L_1 is the amount of labour done in the 'current' period towards the production of the 'current' period wage bundle, w. L_2 is the amount of labour done one period earlier,

L_3 the amount done two periods earlier, etc., etc., towards the production of the 'current' wage bundle. In a stationary economy, L_2, L_3, etc. may equally well be viewed as amounts of labour performed, in the 'current' period, towards the production of the wage bundle paid in the next period, the period after that, etc. In brief, the given real wage bundle, w, and the conditions of production determine the quantities L, L_1, L_2, L_3, ... in (5), and the only unknown therein is thus r. *Hence* (5) *determines the rate of profit*, r, *in terms of known quantities of labour.*[4] With r now determined, relation (3) determines the labour-commanded price of each commodity, again in terms of known quantities of labour.

Dated labour analysis and the physical quantities approach

Before considering some implications of the above analysis, it will be as well to show that that analysis is no more than an alternative presentation of the analysis carried out in the previous chapter. It was shown there – see equation (4) of chapter 4 – that if A be the matrix of material inputs, a the vector of employment by industry, w the real wage bundle and L the total level of employment, then the rate of profit, r, is determined by

$$L = (1+r)a[I - (1+r)A]^{-1}w, \qquad (6)$$

if wages are paid in advance. Now, provided only that wages are not zero and that the production of net output is possible, the matrix on the right-hand side of (6) may be expanded as a power series, to give

$$L = (1+r)a[I + (1+r)A + (1+r)^2A^2 + (1+r)^3A^3 + \ldots]w$$

or

$$L = (1+r)a \cdot w + (1+r)^2 aAw + (1+r)^3 aA^2w + \ldots \qquad (7)$$

In (7), $(a \cdot w)$ is the labour done 'currently' towards the production of the wage bundle, w: (aAw) is the labour done to produce the means of production used in producing w, namely (Aw): (aA^2w) is the labour done to produce the means of production used in making

---

[4] Or, more fundamentally, in terms of production conditions and the wage bundle.

the means of production used to produce w, namely (A^2w): and so on. In other words, (aA^tw) is only a different way of writing what was called L_t above and (5) and (7) are, appearances notwithstanding, identical. Indeed, (5) and (6) are therefore identical – the dated labour analysis is no more than a 'rewriting' of the physical quantities analysis of chapter 4.

Formulation (7) does, however, have the advantage, with respect to (5), of making explicit the fact that the backward resolution of means of production into dated labour quantities is a purely conceptual resolution, and *not* a 'historical story', for it is seen at a glance that the a and A quantities at every step are those of the 'current' period. It also shows why the L_t quantities in (5) eventually tend to zero as t increases, for $L_t \equiv (aA^tw)$ and A^t *must* eventually tend towards the null matrix as t tends to infinity, if the economy in question is to be capable of producing a gross output exceeding the produced inputs used up. (For the same reason, *each* l_{jt} eventually approaches zero.)

Some implications

The real wage bundle, w, will naturally contain many zero elements; workers consume neither ocean-going racing yachts nor sulphuric acid. Ocean-going racers, and similar commodities, can also be assumed not to be used, directly or indirectly, in the production of any commodity which does enter the real wage bundle. It follows that their conditions of production have no influence on the rate of profit, r, as may be seen by noting that a change in those conditions would not cause any change in the *relative* magnitudes of L, L_1, L_2, L_3 . . . in (5). A change in the method of production of sulphuric acid, however, would cause changes in at least some of those quantities if, but only if, it is used, whether directly or indirectly, in producing some commodity entering the wage bundle. The rate of profit depends, as is shown implicitly by (5), only on the real wage bundle and the conditions of its (direct and indirect) production. It does not depend on the conditions of production of 'luxuries' or of any means of production used exclusively in producing them.[5] In other words, the rate of profit depends on just the same factors as does the rate of surplus value (exploitation), though it depends on them in a more complex way, as will now be shown.

It will be clear that, in (5), L may be expressed as $L = V + S$, where V and S are the value of labour power and surplus value respectively. Furthermore, the sum of the L_t quantities is simply V, the amount of labour-time expended, directly or indirectly, in the production of the wage bundle. Thus

$$V = L_1 + L_2 + L_3 + \ldots \tag{8}$$

Now define $k_t \equiv (L_t/V)$, so that k_t is the fraction of V expended $(t-1)$ periods in advance of the availability of the wage bundle. (8) may be rewritten as

$$1 = k_1 + k_2 + k_3 + \ldots; \tag{9}$$

the relative magnitudes of the various k_t express the 'time pattern' of the expenditures of labour-time which sum to V.

Since the rate of exploitation is, by definition, $e \equiv (S/V)$, (5) may now be written, on dividing through by V, as

$$(1+e) = k_1(1+r) + k_2(1+r)^2 + k_3(1+r)^3 + \ldots \tag{10}$$

Since the k_t are non-negative and sum to unity, it follows at once from (10) that r is positive if and only if e is positive and that, for *given* k_t values, e and r are positively related. More important here, however, is the fact that (10) shows clearly the dependence of r on the 'time-pattern' of the expenditures of labour-time making up V. Whereas e depends only on the aggregate magnitude V (given L), r also depends on the 'time-pattern' expressed by $k_1, k_2, \ldots$ To ignore 'constant capital' would amount to setting $k_2 = k_3 = \ldots = 0$ in (10) and thus to arguing that $e = r$. Marx insisted, quite correctly, that constant capital cannot be ignored in the determina-

---

[5] Cf., P. M. Sweezy, *The Theory of Capitalist Development*, London, 1962, pp. 123–4, who points out that this 'result is in accord with Ricardo's theory of profits and Marx's criticism of Ricardo on this score was unjustified'.

tion of the rate of profit but he did not go far enough towards recognizing the full importance of the time-structure of direct and indirect labour inputs. He stopped short at the division between constant capital and variable capital, a division which is not adequate to capture the *whole pattern* of k_t's, which plays a crucial role in determining r.[6][7]

It may be noted finally that in *Capital*, vol. III, Marx states that prices of production depend on the general rate of profit and seems to suggest that this general rate therefore *has* to be deduced *directly* from quantities of labour. 'Without such deduction the general rate of profit (and consequently the price of production of commodities) remains a vague and senseless conception.'[8] *If* the implication is that relating prices to r and r to prices would merely produce a vicious circle, as it appears to be, then Marx is simply wrong. We have *not* deduced r from quantities of labour *independently of prices* but we have nonetheless determined r (and prices of production) in terms of such quantities.

[6] I leave aside the (here) less important point that Marx's C refers to *all* sectors of the economy, some of which, as has been seen, are irrelevant to the determination of r.

[7] Referring to dated labour analysis, Fine and Harris (*op. cit.*, p. 163) write, 'In such a model there is no qualitative difference between dead and living labour, whereas for Marx there is such a difference and it is captured by the concept of value composition.' The first part of this statement is simply false. With respect to the second part it would be better to write that 'In such a model it is seen clearly why Marx's division into constant and variable capital, while a step in the right direction, is not adequate.' Gerstein (*op. cit.*, p. 272) describes as 'ideological' the 'technique of treating constant capital as dated labour'. Presumably the technique of referring to the *sum* of certain dated labour quantities and calling it 'the value of constant capital' is 'scientific'? 'When I make a word do a lot of work like that', said Humpty Dumpty, 'I always pay it extra'.

It may be of interest to note that Marx himself provided a clear explanation of the basic idea of dated labour analysis, in *Capital*, vol. I, *op. cit.*, pp. 294–6 – unfortunately in the inappropriate context of a fixed capital using production process!

[8] Moscow, 1966, p. 157.

Conclusion

The dated labour analysis can be used to show that the rate of profit is determined by the real wage bundle and the conditions of its (direct and indirect) production, being independent of the (direct and indirect) production conditions for 'luxuries'. Such analysis also lays bare the great importance, for the rate of profit, of the *time-structure* of labour inputs (in addition to their total magnitudes) and shows that Marx's division of capital into constant and variable capitals does not suffice to capture that time-structure. It must not be forgotten, however, that dated labour analysis is no substitute for the physical quantities analysis, being derivative of the latter in the case of circulating capital and no joint products and being completely inapplicable when that very special case is left behind. The dated labour analysis is therefore not an essential part of the Sraffa-based critique of Marx.

6

Within the Labour Process

For the most part, it is assumed throughout the present work that there is a fixed relation between the real wage paid to a worker and the amount of work that is actually performed; that relation is 'frozen' simply in order that attention may be focussed on other matters. The various analyses which are based on such a frozen relation will here be supplemented – *but not invalidated* – by an examination of the effects of a thaw.

In this chapter, then, the given real wage will be taken to be the wage paid, by the capitalist, for the use of the worker's capacity to work but while that wage will be held constant, the work actually performed by the worker will be assumed to be variable: it will be seen how the rate of profit depends on the amount and the intensity of work which the capitalist is able to obtain from the worker. While the analysis presented will certainly not *determine* the 'balance of forces' in the workplace, and thus the outcome of coercion and resistance in the labour process,[1] it will show the importance of that balance for the determination of the rate of profit.

Suppose then that a capitalist either has paid or will have to pay[2]

---

[1] *Cf.*, *Capital*, vol. I, chapter 10, 'The Working Day', for an excellent discussion of some of the many economic and political determinants of the length of the working day. See *Capital*, vol. I, *passim*, for the concepts of absolute and relative surplus value, to which the discussion of the present chapter relates. (Of course, 'relative surplus value' refers also to wider aspects of increasing productivity than those considered here.)

[2] According as wages are paid at the beginning or at the end of the period in question.

a given real wage bill for the use of the capacity to work of a given number of workers over some period of time. Other things being equal, the capitalist will seek to;

increase the number of hours worked in that period:
increase the intensity of work by reducing the time taken for any given operation, by reducing any time lapses between successive operations and by squeezing out any general losses of time, whether due to disputes, teabreaks, or any other cause:
reduce the proportion of output which is non-vendible because of inadequate quality:
reduce the use of material inputs per unit of output by enforcing care in avoiding waste:
increase the care with which fixed capital is used.

On the other hand, workers will attempt to resist longer hours and greater intensity of work and, at least beyond a certain point, may also resist pressures towards higher quality output, raw materials saving and care in the use of machinery, when they effectively involve greater intensity of work.[3]

While the effects of coercion and resistance in the labour process could indeed be discussed within the context of the most general analyses presented in this work, the results would be complex; the essential points will therefore be brought out in three *very* simple cases, starting in each case, of course, from a statement of the physical quantities involved in each process of production.[4] These simple examples are presented as no more than illustrations of how the very complex issue of the labour process may be approached in the 'physical quantities' framework.[5]

[3] *Cf.*, Brighton Labour Process Group, 'The Capitalist Labour Process', *Capital and Class*, 1977.

[4] While always ready to assert the importance of analysing the labour process and of 'value analysis', the obscurants are strikingly reticent about *how* they would conduct their analysis *without* starting from the physical quantities involved in production.

[5] The complexity of the issue will be touched on again in Chapter 12.

A very simple economy

Consider a very simple capitalist economy in which there are only two produced commodities, one a produced means of production and the other a wage good. Let the given annual real wage per worker be $\bar{w}$ and the annual rate of profit be r. Wages will be taken to be paid *ex post*,[6] while the price of production of the 'capital good' in terms of the wage good will be denoted by p. There is no *fixed* capital.

Suppose that, in the course of a year's work, a worker either converts 'a' units of the capital good into 'b' saleable units of the capital good or converts 'A' units of the capital good into 'B' saleable units of the wage good. Then

$$(1+r)ap + \bar{w} = bp \qquad (1)$$

and

$$(1+r)Ap + \bar{w} = B, \qquad (2)$$

where (1) refers to capital good production and (2) to wage good production. It follows from (1) and (2) that:

$$(1+r) = \left[\frac{b(B - \bar{w})}{aB + (A - a)\bar{w}} \right] \qquad (3)$$

The annual wage being held constant at $\bar{w}$, (3) may now be used to examine the effects on the profit rate, r, of changes in hours of work, intensity of work, etc., effects which will, of course, be transmitted through the corresponding changes in 'a', 'b', 'A' and 'B'.

If the annual hours of work are increased, from any initial level, the physical quantities of inputs processed and outputs produced will also increase, that is 'a', 'b', 'A' and 'B' will all rise. If workers are to continue to work in both industries, in the long run, then it must be assumed that hours increase in the same proportion in each industry, since workers would otherwise leave the industry with the

---

[6] Taking wages to be paid *ex ante* would make no real difference to the conclusions reached but would make their expression far more tortuous.

greater percentage increase in hours. Such a proportionate increase in *hours* would not necessarily give rise to an equi-proportional increase in the *outputs*, 'b' and 'B', but in order to isolate the effect of longer hours from effects discussed below, it may be assumed that hours and output do indeed increase in the same proportion as each other and as between industries. For the same reason, it may be assumed that inputs consumed will also rise in the same proportion.

Similarly, an overall increase in the intensity of work, whatever the precise form of the intensification involved, would mean that 'a', 'b', 'A' and 'B' all rise, even if total *hours* of work are constant. Again, although the concept of intensity of work is difficult to render precise, it can be said that the increase in 'intensity' in each industry must be such that neither industry will lose its workers. In order to capture the effects of a pure, overall increase in intensity, it may again be assumed that 'a', 'b', 'A' and 'B' all increase in the same proportion.

By contrast, pressure on the workers to raise the proportion of products which meet the necessary quality specification for a vendible commodity, may result in increases in 'b' and 'B' without any corresponding increases in 'a' and 'A', while successful pressure for the saving of raw materials[7] may decrease 'a' and 'A' without decreasing 'b' and 'B'.

The above statements, it need hardly be said, are all *ceteris paribus* statements: there is no reason at all why capitalists should not simultaneously seek to lengthen hours of work, intensify the pace of work, improve quality and save raw materials, nor why workers should not be resisting various such changes simultaneously.

As has been said above, both an overall increase in hours and a pure, overall increase in the intensity of work may be assumed to produce equi-proportionate increases in 'a', 'b', 'A' and 'B'. Suppose then that, due to an increase in hours and/or an increase in the overall intensity of work, the levels of material input and output

---

[7] Pressure for careful use of fixed capital, which obviously cannot be discussed in the present context, will be referred to below.

increase from 'a', 'b', 'A' and 'B' to '$(1+k)a$', '$(1+k)b$', '$(1+k)A$' and '$(1+k)B$' respectively, where 100k is, of course, the percentage increase in each quantity. Replacing each of the four quantities in (3) by the corresponding new, increased quantity, one finds that (3) is changed to

$$(1+r) = \left[\frac{b[B-\overline{w}/(1+k)]}{aB+(A-a)\overline{w}/(1+k)} \right]. \tag{4}$$

Now (4) is just the same as (3), except that $\overline{w}$ in (3) is replaced by $[\overline{w}/(1+k)]$ in (4). In other words, *the effect on the rate of profit* of a $k\%$ overall increase in hours and/or intensity of work, with a given wage, is just the same as the effect of a $k\%$ wage cut, with given hours and intensity of work, i.e., to increase the rate of profit. (Which is not, of course, to say that an increase in hours and/or intensity is the same thing as a real wage cut.) The real wage being given then, capitalists have every incentive to lengthen the hours and increase the intensity of work; while workers have every reason to resist such changes and, indeed, to push for reductions in hours and in work intensity.

On the other hand, increases in output with given material inputs or decreases in the use of material inputs with given levels of outputs, while they certainly increase the rate of profit, are not even formally equivalent to a real wage cut. Thus if, for example, output levels of vendible commodities are increased by $100m\%$, i.e. from 'b' and 'B' to '$(1+m)b$' and '$(1+m)B$', respectively, while inputs 'a' and 'A' remain constant, then on substituting the new output quantities into (3) one finds that

$$(1+r) = (1+m)\left[\frac{b[B-\overline{w}/(1+m)]}{aB+(A-a)\overline{w}/(1+m)} \right]. \tag{5}$$

Hence the effect of a $100m\%$ increase in outputs, with given material inputs, has the same effect on the rate of profit as a $100m\%$ real wage cut – $\overline{w}$ in (3) is replaced by $\overline{w}/(1+m)$ in (5) – *together with* an overall rise of $100m\%$ in 'one plus the rate of profit' – the expression between [ ] on the right-hand side of (5) is multiplied by $(1+m)$.

Thus from the capitalists' point of view, an overall percentage increase in output, holding real wages and material inputs constant, is more desirable than an equal percentage cut in real wages, holding output and material input levels constant.

Finally, if capitalists can enforce a reduction in the material input quantities from 'a' and 'A' to, say, 'a/(1+n)' and 'A/(1+n)', respectively, with real wages and output levels unchanged, then (3) is simply changed to

$$(1+r) = (1+n)\left[\frac{b(B-\bar{w})}{aB+(A-a)\bar{w}}\right] \qquad (6)$$

'One plus the rate of profit' in (6) is just $(1+n)$ times the corresponding term in (3).[8]

Suppose, briefly, that a third, 'luxury', commodity is also produced, 'α' units of the capital good being transformed into 'β' units of this luxury good. If the production price of the latter, in terms of the wage good, be π, (1) and (2) will then be supplemented by the relation

$$(1+r)\alpha p + \bar{v} = \beta\pi$$

but (1) and (2) will still suffice to determine r as in (3). Thus variations in α and β, while they will affect π, *will have no effect on* r.

(While the above analysis has naturally been focussed on the rate of profit, relations (1) and (2) can also be used to determine the price of production, p, as

$$p = \left[\frac{aB+(A-a)\bar{w}}{Ab}\right]$$

The interested reader will have no difficulty in analysing the effects of the above mentioned changes within the labour process on this price of production.)

Of greater interest, perhaps, is the question how such changes

[8] It may be noted that, *ceteris paribus*, a given percentage increase in output levels is thus equivalent, *in its effect on the rate of profit*, to an equal percentage wage cut combined with an equal percentage reduction in material input use.

affect the rate of surplus value. Suppose that workers spend h hours using 'a' to produce 'b' and H hours using 'A' to produce 'B'. Let l and L be the hours of labour required, directly and indirectly, to produce one unit of net output of the capital good and of the wage good, respectively.[9] Marx's 'c + v + s' value accounts may thus be written as

$$al + h = bl \tag{7}$$

and

$$Al + H = BL. \tag{8}$$

It follows from (7) and (8) that

$$L = \left[\frac{Ah + (b-a)H}{B(b-a)} \right] \tag{9}$$

Now if the total real wage bill is denoted by $\bar{w}$, total surplus value, S, and total variable capital, V, are given by

$$S = (h + H) - \bar{w} \cdot L \tag{10}$$

and

$$V = \bar{w} \cdot L \tag{11}$$

Defining the rate of surplus value (and rate of exploitation) as $e \equiv (S/V)$, it follows from (9), (10) and (11) that

$$(1 + e) = \left(\frac{h + H}{\bar{w}} \right) \cdot \left[\frac{B(b-a)}{Ah + (b-a)H} \right]. \tag{12}$$

It is now easy to show, from (12), that if, say, all the quantities on the right of (12) other than the wage bill, $\bar{w}$ (hours, material inputs, outputs) are increased in the same proportion, then $(1 + e)$ will also increase in that proportion.

On the other hand, if outputs, 'b' and 'B', are increased, *ceteris*

---

[9] The reader will not have forgotten that *under our background assumptions,* set out in chapter 1, l and L may, without danger of confusion, be called the 'values' of the respective commodities.

84

paribus, or if inputs, 'a' and 'A', are decreased, *ceteris paribus*, e will certainly increase but will not do so proportionately. The reader may pursue the matter as desired.

A generalization
The above very simple analysis can readily be generalized to the case of n commodities, retaining the assumptions of no fixed capital and no pure joint products. Let the vector w be the annual wage expressed as a bundle of commodities, r be the annual rate of profit and p be the vector of prices of production. If A is the (n × n) matrix of annual material inputs and Q is the diagonal (n × n) matrix of annual outputs, then, if wages are paid in advance,

$$(1+r)p(A + w \cdot i) = pQ, \tag{13}$$

where i is a row vector, all of whose elements are unity. It follows immediately from (13) that $(1+r)^{-1}$ is the Perron–Frobenius root of the non-negative matrix,

$$M \equiv (A + w \cdot i)Q^{-1}.$$

Remembering that the maximal root of M is positively related – and hence that r is *inversely* related – to every element of M,[10] one may now generalize the various results obtained above, concerning the effects of changes in the labour process on the rate of profit.

Fixed capital
A very simple capitalist economy in which fixed capital is used may now be considered. There is one kind of machine. One machine has to be operated by one worker and it can be used to produce either machines or the wage good; in either type of production process, it

[10] If M is reducible then 'positively' and '*inversely*' must be taken in the weak sense – but *still* hold in the strong sense with respect to the elements of the irreducible square matrix at the top left-hand corner of M, when the latter has been reduced as far as possible.

lasts for just two years, operating with constant efficiency.

Let the annual wage per worker be $\bar{w}$, and the annual rate of profit be r, while P and p denote the production prices, in terms of the wage good, of a new machine and a one-year old machine, respectively.[11] If, using one machine, a worker produces either m machines or q units of the wage good in a year, then

$$(1+r)P + \bar{w} = mP + p \tag{14}$$

$$(1+r)P + \bar{w} = q + p \tag{15}$$

$$(1+r)p + \bar{w} = mP \tag{16}$$

$$(1+r)p + \bar{w} = q. \tag{17}$$

It will be noted that in (14) and (15), which refer to production processes using the new machine, the production price of the old machine is entered on the right-hand side.[12] It follows from (14) to (17) that

$$\left[\frac{(1+r)^2}{2+r}\right] = \left(\frac{m}{q}\right)(q - \bar{w}) \tag{18}$$

$$P = \left(\frac{q}{m}\right) \tag{19}$$

$$p = \left(\frac{1+r}{2+r}\right)\left(\frac{q}{m}\right) \tag{20}$$

Suppose now that a worker is forced to produce more in a year, whether by working longer or by working harder. The annual outputs, q and/or m, will rise and thus the right-hand side of (18) will increase. Since the expression on the left-hand side of (18) increases as r increases, it follows that an increase in q and/or m will lead to a rise in the rate of profit, r. Thus, again, capitalists have every interest in increasing the hours and the intensity of work, as long as such increases cause output to rise. (If pushed too far, longer

[11] The price of a two-year old machine is zero, there being no 'scrap value'.
[12] See below, chapters 10, 12, 13 (especially chapter 10).

and more intense work might actually lead to a drop in annual output and thus to a *fall* in the rate of profit.)

More specifically, if output levels increase proportionately, from m and q to $(1+k)m$ and $(1+k)q$, respectively, it is clear from (18) that r increases. (The production price of a new machine, P, will be unaffected; *cf.* (19). The production price of the one-year old machine, p, however, will rise – *cf.* (20) – for (q/m) will be unchanged, while $[(1+r)/(2+r)]$ will rise.)

Thus far, nothing has been said about pressure on workers to take care of fixed capital. To indicate, in a *very* brief and simple way, how this question may be analysed, it may be supposed that, the other assumptions being unchanged, the machine lasts t years. It is easy to show that (18) is then modified to

$$\left[\frac{r(1+r)^t}{(1+r)^t - 1} \right] = \left(\frac{m}{q} \right) \cdot (q - \bar{w}). \tag{21}$$

Now the left-hand side of (21) is a decreasing function of t and an increasing function of r, so that if workers can be made to use the machines more carefully and thus increase t, then the profit rate, r, will be increased, for given values of m, q and $\bar{w}$.

In practice, of course, there will be an interaction between this issue and that discussed immediately above, for if workers work more hours and/or more intensely each year, then this will generally decrease the number of years for which a machine remains usable. Thus, in (21), m and q will be *increasing* functions of hours worked and of the intensity of work, at least up to a certain point, while t will be a *decreasing* function of hours and of intensity. The capitalists will thus try to discover – and to enforce – the profit rate maximizing combination of hours per year and intensity of work; which is not, of course, to say that they will necessarily succeed.

Conclusion

The above examples, though exceedingly simple,[13] should suffice to

[13] Once the general approach has been grasped, the reader will be able to

indicate the effects of longer hours, speed up, raw materials saving, greater care of machinery, etc., on the rate of profit – and thus why such objectives are pursued by capitalists. They also show that such issues can be analysed by starting from a statement of the physical quantities of material inputs and outputs: suggestions to the effect that the Sraffa framework[14] can be used *only* for the analysis of the relations between wages, profits and prices, and can contribute nothing to the analysis of changes within the labour process, are simply false.

---

analyse more complex cases. The examples given above are intended to do no more than point the way.

[14] Sraffa, in *Production of Commodities, etc.*, did not discuss changes in the labour process; nor did he need to do so, given the precise purpose of that work.

7

Heterogeneous Labour

The assumption is generally made throughout this work that, while different kinds of concrete labour necessarily differ one from another, any worker can perform each type of concrete labour; since workers are mobile between industries this means, in turn, that real wages are uniform throughout the abstract capitalist economies considered. In the present chapter, however, that assumption will be relaxed and it will be shown how surplus labour and profits can be analysed in the presence of heterogeneous labour, *without any need to 'reduce' one kind of labour-time to another.*[1]

Marxist discussions of the 'reduction' of various labour-times to one 'simple' labour-time, generally take place in the context of skilled and unskilled labour and the following analysis can indeed be taken to refer to that context. Yet it need not be so interpreted. One effect of skill differentials is, of course, to give rise to real wage differentials but the latter do not necessarily spring from the former. Various kinds of discrimination and restriction of access to particular jobs[2] can create semi-permanent wage differentials which bear no relation to objective differences in skill requirements. The different kinds of labour considered below may thus refer to skill grades and/or to 'artificial differentiation' of labour.[3]

---

[1] This chapter is based on material presented to a conference on 'Wages Theory' at the I.D.S., University of Sussex, in 1975.

[2] E.g., discrimination on grounds of sex or race.

[3] It need hardly be said that the line between 'skill differences' and 'artificial differences' may sometimes be decidedly blurred, both because skill grades

Two kinds of labour

Consider first a capitalist economy in which there are two types of labour-time, the real wage rates for which are given by the two bundles of commodities w_1 and w_2, where w_1 and w_2 are column vectors with n components if there are n commodities produced. Let the n element row vector l_1 show the amounts of type one labour-time required, directly or indirectly, for the production of single units of the various commodities; let l_2 be defined analogously.[4] It follows from these definitions that the production of the real wage bundle paid for one unit of type one labour-time requires, directly or indirectly, the expenditure of $(l_1 \cdot w_1)$ units of type one labour-time *and* the expenditure of $(l_2 \cdot w_1)$ units of type two labour-time. In the same way, $(l_1 \cdot w_2)$ and $(l_2 \cdot w_2)$ units of type one and type two labour-time, respectively, are required for the production of the real wage paid for one unit of type two labour-time.

Suppose now that E_1 and E_2 units of the two kinds of labour are employed in the economy. The amount of type one labour expended in the production of real wages, *whether paid to type one or to type two labour*, will then be $[(l_1 \cdot w_1)E_1 + (l_1 \cdot w_2)E_2]$. In the same way, the amount of type two labour expended in producing real wages, for either kind of labour, will be $[(l_2 \cdot w_1)E_1 + (l_2 \cdot w_2)E_2]$. Now, if there are to be profits, some labour of each type must be directed to the production of the commodities appropriated by the capitalists (whether for consumption or accumulation purposes). More pre-

---

may be preserved after the period in which they had an objective significance and because discrimination will often take the form of denying access to the acquisition of objective skills or of insisting on the possession of irrelevant, pseudo-skills. For an extended discussion of the background issues, and for a bibliography which includes references to empirical studies, see S. Bowles and H. Gintis, 'The Marxian Theory of Value and Heterogeneous Labour: A Critique and Reformulation', *Cambridge Journal of Economics*, 1977.

[4] It will be assumed, for simplicity, that each of l_1, l_2 is *strictly* positive, i.e., that each kind of labour is required, directly or indirectly, for the production of every commodity. The reader may relax this assumption. Constant returns to scale are assumed in this chapter.

cisely, there will be positive profits if and only if[5]

$$(l_1 \cdot w_1)E_1 + (l_1 \cdot w_2)E_2 < E_1 \qquad (1)$$

and

$$(l_2 \cdot w_1)E_1 + (l_2 \cdot w_2)E_2 < E_2 \qquad (2)$$

For surplus labour *of each type* will then be performed.

Given that all the terms involved in (1) and (2) are positive, it is immediately apparent that a *necessary* condition for the satisfaction of (1) and (2) is that

$$(l_1 \cdot w_1) < 1 \qquad (3)$$

and

$$(l_2 \cdot w_2) < 1 \qquad (4)$$

Relation (3) says that less than one unit of type one labour-time must be required for the production of the real wage paid for one unit of type one labour-time; (4) makes the corresponding statement with respect to type two labour.

However, while conditions (3) and (4) are certainly *necessary* if there is to be surplus labour for the production of commodities for the capitalists, they are by no means *sufficient*. For each type of labour-time is expended in producing real wages not only for the workers who expend it *but also for the other kind of workers*. To find the sufficient condition for the existence of profits, it may be noted that, given the satisfaction of (3) and (4), (1) and (2) imply that

$$\left[\frac{(l_1 \cdot w_2)}{1 - (l_1 \cdot w_1)} \right] < \left(\frac{E_1}{E_2} \right) < \left[\frac{1 - (l_2 \cdot w_2)}{(l_2 \cdot w_1)} \right] \qquad (5)$$

and hence that

$$[1 - (l_1 \cdot w_1)][1 - (l_2 \cdot w_2)] > (l_1 \cdot w_2) \cdot (l_2 \cdot w_1) \qquad (6)$$

---

[5] A more direct analysis, in terms of the rate of profit and prices of production, will be found later in this chapter and in chapter 12.

It will be clear that the satisfaction of (3) and (4) does not suffice to guarantee the satisfaction of (6). The necessary and sufficient condition for the *possibility* of profits is thus that (3), (4) and (6) all be satisfied.[6] Profits will actually exist if, in addition to (3), (4) and (6) being satisfied, the relative employment levels satisfy condition (5).

If there were only one kind of labour, with real wage rate w and vector of direct and indirect labour requirements l, the condition for the existence of profits would, of course, be simply

$$(l \cdot w) < 1. \qquad (7)[7]$$

It will be clear that (3), (4) and (6) merely generalize condition (7) to the case of two types of labour. Conditions (3) and (4) are directly analogous to (7), while the further condition (6) takes account of the fact that workers of each kind have to expend labour not only in producing their own real wages but also in producing the real wages of the other kind of workers 'before', so to speak, they expend labour in producing commodities for capitalists. While the analysis is a little more complicated with two kinds of labour than with one, it is thus straightforward to show the conditions for the extraction of surplus labour, of each type, without any need to 'reduce' one kind of labour to another.

Many kinds of labour

Now let there be N kinds of labour, let w_j be the real wage for one unit of type j labour and let l_i be the vector of direct and indirect use of type i labour. Define the square, $N \times N$, matrix V by $v_{ij} = (l_i \cdot w_j)$, i.e., the ij^{th} element of V shows the amount of type i labour used in the production of the real wage for one unit of type j labour. If the $(N \times n)$ matrix L has l_i as its ith row and the $(n \times N)$ matrix W has w_j as its jth column then, of course, $V \equiv LW$. It will be assumed, for simplicity, that the non-negative matrix $V \equiv LW$ is irreducible.

---

[6] Of course, either of (3) and (4), together with (6), implies the other.
[7] I.e., it takes less than one unit of labour to produce the real wage paid for one unit of labour.

The production of commodities for the capitalists is possible in this system if and only if there exists a semi-positive vector of employment levels, E, such that

$$VE + S = E \qquad (8)$$

where S is any given semi-positive vector of surplus labour quantities, defined by $S = LC$, C being the vector of commodities appropriated by the capitalists. Re-writing (8) as

$$E = (I - V)^{-1}S \qquad (9)$$

it will be seen that profits can exist if and only if $(I - V)^{-1}$ is a 'Leontief inverse' matrix. The condition for the possibility of producing commodities for the capitalists – i.e. for the possibility of profits – is thus that the Perron–Frobenius root of V should be less than unity. Writing this condition as

$$\lambda^{PF}(V) = \lambda^{PF}(LW) < 1 \qquad (10)$$

it will be clear that (10) is the generalization, for the case of N types of labour, of the usual condition (7). It thus provides a compact statement of the relations between labour use and real wages which must obtain, in a N labour type capitalist economy, if that economy is to be viable on a capitalist basis, i.e., to generate positive profits. *It does not involve any 'reduction' of one kind of labour to another.*

The rate of profit

It may now be considered briefly how the rate of profit is determined in a simple capitalist economy with n single-product industries and N kinds of labour. Let the gross output of each commodity be unity by a suitable choice of physical units of measurement; let M be the $n \times n$ matrix of material input quantities and A be the $N \times n$ matrix, the jth row of which, a_j, shows the quantities of the jth kind of labour used in the various industries.[8]

---

[8] The L matrix referred to above is given by $L \equiv A(I - M)^{-1}$.

If m_j is the money wage rate of type j labour, paid in advance, r is the annual rate of profit and p^m is the row vector of money prices of commodities, then

$$(1+r)(p^mM + m_1a_1 + m_2a_2 + \ldots + m_Na_N) = p^m \qquad (11)$$

Now if the real wage bundle for one unit of type j labour is w_j (and workers do no saving) then

$$m_j = p^m \cdot w_j \qquad (12)$$

Then, using (12) to eliminate the m_j's from (11), one obtains

$$(1+r)p^m(M + w_1 \cdot a_1 + w_2 \cdot a_2 + \ldots + w_N \cdot a_N) = p^m \qquad (13)$$

If the semi-positive matrix on the left-hand side of (13) is assumed to be irreducible, then it follows at once that $(1+r)^{-1}$ is the Perron–Frobenius root of that matrix.[9] The rate of profit is thus determined, by the physical inputs and outputs, by the real wage bundles and by the direct uses of different kinds of labour in the various industries. That determination involves no reference to 'reduction' of different kinds of labour-time, nor indeed to *any* concept of direct and indirect labour use.

Conclusion

The existence of heterogeneous labour, for whatever reason, creates no essential problem for the analysis of surplus labour, nor for the determination of the rate of profit. In each case the process of 'reduction' is completely redundant.

Appendix

It was seen above, in (9), that

$$E = (I - V)^{-1}S.$$

[9] The matrix in question may be written as $(M + WA)$; $\lambda^{PF}(M + WA) < 1$ is thus the condition for a positive rate of profit. The rate of profit will decrease

Thus only if, by a fluke, $S \equiv LC$ should be a characteristic vector of $V \equiv LW$ (associated with its Perron–Frobenius root) will E and S be proportional. Consequently, *if* the rate of exploitation of type j labour, e_j, is defined by

$$e_j \equiv \left(\frac{S_j}{E_j - S_j} \right)$$

then that rate will differ, in general, from one kind of labour to another and will, indeed, depend on the relative magnitudes of the elements of $S \equiv LC$, and thus on the composition of C. (If 'e' *is* uniform then $(1+e)^{-1} = \lambda^{PF}(LW)$.)

Whether the rate of exploitation for type j labour should be defined in this way – where the denominator is type j labour expended in the production of *all* wage goods – what the definition should be if not this one and whether the existence of a differential rate is held to constitute a 'problem' in any sense, are questions which will be left for the reader's consideration. *The answers given to them do not affect the truth of what is said in the main text of this chapter.*

---

as *any* element of *any* real wage bundle is increased. Its dependence on hours worked, speed-up, etc., may be analysed as shown in chapter 6. See also chapter 12.

8

Miscellanea

This chapter draws together a number of different discussions which, while perhaps of some interest in their own right, are not of central importance to the principal arguments of this work; they may, nevertheless, serve as useful further illustrations of those arguments, since they each bring out, once again, the crucial role of the physically specified methods of production and real wages. After some further discussion of the rate of profit, the effects of differential wages and of the timing of wage payments will be examined. The relationship between real wages and the rate of exploitation, in the presence of a choice of technique, will then be considered, as will the role of value magnitudes in constraining the *physical composition* of capitalists' profits. It will then be shown, finally, how 'pure circulation' activities may be analysed, using the physical quantities approach advocated throughout this work.

Further on the rate of profit

It was seen in the example of chapter 3 and, more generally, in chapter 4 that, in the conventional notation, $(S/C + V)$ is not the rate of profit in a capitalist economy. Confusion over this issue being so well entrenched, it may be useful to reiterate the point from a slightly different perspective, that of the maximum possible rate of profit, i.e., the (purely notional) rate of profit which would be obtained if

95

wages were zero.[1]

If wages were zero, the rate of profit according to Marx's (incorrect) formulation would be given by $(S + V/C)$, i.e. by the ratio of total living labour to total embodied (past) labour. In the example of chapter 3, total living labour $(S + V)$, was equal to 80, while total embodied labour, C, was equal to 112 (see Table II). Hence, according to Marx's formula, the maximum possible rate of profit was $(S + V/C) = 80/112 = 71.43\%$ approximately.

However, Table I of chapter 3 shows that if wages were zero, while total inputs and outputs remained unchanged, the rate of profit, R, would be given by

$$(1 + R)28P_i = 56P_i \tag{1}$$

$$(1 + R)16P_i = 48 \tag{2}$$

$$(1 + R)12P_i = 8P_c \tag{3}$$

where P_i and P_c are the corresponding gold prices of a unit of iron and a unit of corn, respectively. Equation (1) suffices to determine R as

$$R = 100\%, \tag{4}$$

while (2) and (3) then yield $P_i = 1.5$ and $P_c = 4.5$. Thus, in this particular example, Marx's formula greatly under-estimates the (hypothetical) maximum possible rate of profit.

That Marx's formula can equally well over-estimate the maximum possible rate of profit can be shown from the example given in Table I below.

Table I

	Tools	Labour		Tools	Corn
	3	4	→	4	–
	1	4	→	–	4
Total	4	8	→	4	4

[1] Or, as Marx put it, if workers 'could live on air', *Capital*, vol. III, chapter 15, section 2 (Moscow, 1966 edition, p. 247).

In the tool industry, 4 units of labour-time use 3 tools to make 4 tools; in the corn industry, 4 units of labour-time use 1 tool to make 4 units of corn. Since tools are assumed to last for only one production cycle, in either industry, total output of tools equals the total number of tools used up and thus the economy is in a state of simple reproduction, provided that, in every period, the net product of 4 units of corn is divided in the same way between workers and capitalists. The (hypothetical) maximum possible wage rate is clearly $(\frac{4}{8}) = (\frac{1}{2})$ a unit of corn per unit of labour-time.

The values of a tool and of a unit of corn, l_t and l_c, are, from Table I, given by

$$3l_t + 4 = 4l_t$$

and

$$l_t + 4 = 4l_c$$

or

$$l_t = 4, \ l_c = 2.$$

Thus if the real corn wage rate is w, where $0 \leq w \leq \frac{1}{2}$, Table I may be converted into the table of value accounts, Table II, in which W shows the value of gross output in each row.

Table II

C	V	S	W
12 +	8w +	(4–8w) =	16
4 +	8w +	(4–8w) =	8

Total			
16 +	16w +	(8–16w) =	24

(V is equal to 8w in each industry since the real corn wage bill is 4w and each unit of corn embodies 2 units of labour, so that $V = 4w \times 2 = 8w$.) Marx's formula for the rate of profit then gives

$$\left(\frac{S}{C+V}\right) = \left(\frac{8-16w}{16+16w}\right) = \left(\frac{0.5-w}{1+w}\right). \tag{5}$$

As may be seen from (5), or from the last row of Table II, according to Marx's formula the maximum possible rate of profit, with w = 0, is given by

$$\left(\frac{S+V}{C}\right) = \left(\frac{8}{16}\right) = 50\%.$$

In fact, the first two rows of Table I show that the maximum possible rate of profit, R, is given by

$$(1+R)3P_t = 4P_t \tag{6}$$

and

$$(1+R)P_t = 4, \tag{7}$$

where P_t is the corresponding exchange value of a tool in terms of corn. Relations (6) and (7) yield:

$$R = 33\tfrac{1}{3}\%, \; P_t = 3.$$

Thus, in this example, Marx's formula, $(S+V/C)$, greatly over-estimates the maximum possible rate of profit, R. Indeed it follows from (5) that

$$\left(\frac{S}{C+V}\right) > R$$

for all wage rates, w, such that $0 \leqq w < \tfrac{1}{8}$. Even for a positive real wage, Marx's formula can give a profit rate which is actually greater than the maximum possible profit rate (corresponding to a zero real wage)!

[The correct determination of the profit rate, r, in the present example is, of course, provided by the relations, obtained from the first two rows of Table I,

$$(1+r)(3p_t + 4w) = 4p_t$$

and

$$(1+r)(p_t + 4w) = 4,$$

where p_t is the exchange value of a tool in terms of corn. It follows that $p_t = (2/1 - r)$, where r is the smaller root of

$$(2w)r^2 - 3r + (1 - 2w) = 0.]$$

It is shown in Table I that 3 tools are needed to make 4 tools. Thus, if there are constant returns to scale, the maximum possible rate at which the stock of tools can be expanded is $[(4-3)/3] = 33\frac{1}{3}\%$. 'One-third' is the highest technically possible growth rate in the economy shown in Table I, the achievement of that (hypothetical) growth rate requiring that no corn is produced, with workers 'living on air' and the capitalists re-investing all their profits.[2] Yet it has been seen that, with $w < \frac{1}{8}$, $(S/C + V)$ exceeds one-third. How then could one be led to 'emphasise movements in the value rate of profit as the critical indicator of the ability of capitalist society to create the conditions for a continued accumulation, free of economic and social crisis'?[3]

Differential wages

It was shown in chapter 7 that the presence of heterogeneous labour need cause no difficulties for the concept of 'surplus labour', whether the labour force is segmented by skills or by other factors, there

---

[2] Of course, it is not a coincidence that this maximum growth rate is equal to the maximum profit rate: such an equality obtains in any economic system of the type considered here.

[3] Fine and Harris, *op. cit.*, p. 154. Without realizing it, Fine and Harris have here answered their own question (p. 151), 'Why is the price (rather than value) rate of profit . . . a central concept for understanding capitalist development?' Their suggestion, *ibid*, that the rationale for focusing on 'the price rate of profit' involves regarding individual behaviour propensities as more fundamental than underlying social forces is mere rhetoric: it is precisely the competitive economic structure of capitalist societies which forces capitalists always to seek the highest money rate of profit. (Marx was, of course, perfectly clear that it is not in the least asocial or astructural to assert that the capitalist's subjective aim is that of maximum accumulation; *Capital*, vol. I, chapter 24, section 3, *op. cit.*, pp. 738–46.) It is strange that anyone should still be confusing this issue seventy years after Bortkiewicz explained the matter perfectly clearly (*op. cit.*, p. 23).

being no need in either case to 'reduce' one kind of labour to another
It will now be considered, first in a very simple case with two kind
of labour and then in a more general case, how the uniform rate o
profit is related to the different real wage rates paid for differen
kinds of heterogeneous labour.

Consider first a very simple capitalist economy in which the only
two products are a single produced means of production and a single
consumption good, gross output of each commodity being unity by
a suitable choice of units. The inputs to the 'producer good' industry
are 'a' units of means of production, b_1 units of type 1 labour and b.
units of type 2 labour; the corresponding inputs to the 'consumer
good' industry are 'A', B_1 and B_2 respectively.[4] If the produced
means of production is entirely used up in one year's production, in
either industry, then the annual rate of profit, r, the real wage rates
for the two kinds of labour, w_1 and w_2 (both paid at the end of the
year) and the relative price of a unit of means of production in terms
of a unit of the consumer good, p, are related by:

$$(1+r)ap + b_1w_1 + b_2w_2 = p \tag{8}$$

and

$$(1+r)Ap + B_1w_1 + B_2w_2 = 1. \tag{9}$$

It follows immediately from (8) and (9), when p is eliminated, that

$$[B_1 + (Ab_1 - aB_1)(1+r)]w_1 + [B_2 + (Ab_2 - aB_2)(1+r)]w_2$$
$$= [1 - a(1+r)]. \tag{10}$$

It is not difficult to show, from (10), that holding either real wage
rate constant, r is inversely related to the other real wage rate. It
follows, of course, that for any given value of the profit rate, r, the
real wage rates, w_1 and w_2 are inversely related. (More precisely, it
can be seen from (10) that for any given value of r there is an inverse
linear relation between w_1 and w_2.) The possible combinations of

---

[4] If $A + a = 1$, and b_1, b_2, B_1 and B_2 are constant from period to period,
then the economy will be undergoing simple reproduction.

r, w_1 and w_2 are shown in Figure 1.[5] An increase in the real wage

Figure I

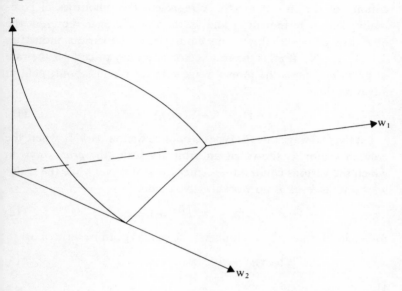

rate of one group of workers need not necessarily lead to a fall in the rate of profit – it might lead to a fall in the real wage rate of the other group of workers instead, or, of course, to a fall in *both* the profit rate and the other real wage rate, etc. (The one thing it could not lead to would be a rise in both the profit rate and the other real wage rate – unless technical progress were brought about.) The *actual* outcome resulting from such an increase cannot be predicted at the present level of abstraction, it need hardly be said, since that will depend on many matters not considered here.

[5] While the exact curvatures of the surface in Figure I are not important for our present purpose, it may be noted that the figure has been drawn on the assumption that $(Ab_1/B_1) < a < (Ab_2^\cdot/B_2)$.

To see, now, that just the same kind of conclusions hold in a more general case, consider a simple capitalist economy, with no fixed capital and no pure joint products, in which the gross output of each of n commodities is unity, by a suitable choice of units. Let the jth column of the $(n \times n)$ matrix A represent the quantities of commodity inputs in industry j and let the row vector a_i represent the quantities of type i labour-time employed in the various industries $(i = 1, \ldots, N)$. If p^m is the row vector of money prices, r is the rate of profit and m_i is the money wage rate for type i labour, paid in advance, then

$$(1+r)(p^m A + \Sigma_1^N m_i a_i) = p^m. \tag{11}$$

Let the real wage rate for type i labour be written as $w_i w_i$, where the column vector w_i shows, at an arbitrary scale, the *proportions* in which the various commodities enter the real wage, while the scalar w_i shows its *level*. If no workers save then

$$m_i = w_i(p^m \cdot w_i), \tag{12}$$

for each i. Using (12) to eliminate the m_i, (11) can be written as

$$(1+r)p^m[A + \Sigma_1^N w_i(w_i \cdot a_i)] = p^m. \tag{13}$$

Hence

$$(1+r)^{-1} = \lambda^{PF}[A + \Sigma_1^N w_i(w_i \cdot a_i)]. \tag{14}$$

Relation (14) determines the rate of profit in terms of the physical conditions of production $(A, a_1, \ldots, a_N)$ and the real wage rates $(w_1 w_1, \ldots, w_N w_N)$. No question of 'reduction' of the different kinds of labour arises, of course, as was seen before in chapter 7.

If the square, semi-positive matrix on the right of (14) is irreducible, then r is inversely related to each w_i. It follows at once that, for given values of r and any $(N-2)$ of the real wage levels w_i, the remaining two real wage levels are inversely related.

Other things being equal, there are potential conflicts between the real wage levels of different groups of workers. (Anyone inclined to leap to any immediate political conclusions on the basis of that fact should think again.)

The timing of wage payments

It was remarked in chapter 1 that excessive importance is sometimes attached to the question whether wages should be assumed to be advanced or to be paid at the end of the production period; this confusion perhaps arises because Marx both generally analysed the rate of profit under the assumption of *advanced* wages and pointed out expressly that the worker is usually paid *after* working for the contracted period.[6] The fact is, of course, that the period of production is generally longer than the period over which the wage contract is made, so it is true both that workers are paid at the end of the wage contract period and that most wages have to be paid before the end of the production period.

To illustrate the general manner in which this issue may be analysed, consider a production process, involving no fixed capital and a single product, which takes one year. The gross output is one unit of the commodity in question. All the produced means of production are purchased by the capitalist at the beginning of the year but wages are paid weekly, at the end of each week.[7] Let the money value of the means of production be c^m, the total *annual* money wage bill be v^m, the money price of the commodity be p^m and the annual and weekly rates of profit be r and r_w respectively. By definition

$$(1 + r_w)^{52} \equiv (1 + r). \tag{15}$$

Now if wages are paid in a constant stream of payments, equal to $(v^m/52)$ at the *end* of each week we must have:

$$(1 + r)c^m + \left(\frac{v^m}{52}\right)[1 + (1 + r_w) + (1 + r_w)^2 + \ldots + (1 + r_w)^{51}] = p^m. \tag{16}$$

[6] *Cf., Capital,* vol. I, chapter 6, *op. cit.,* p. 278.
[7] The 'year' consists of exactly 52 weeks, i.e. 364 days, and no holidays, etc. make any difference to the pattern of wage payments.

Since the sum of the geometric series in the square bracket on the left of (16) is equal to

$$\left[\frac{(1+r_w)^{52}-1}{(1+r_w)-1}\right],$$

(16) may be rewritten, taking account of (15), as

$$(1+r)c^m+\left(\frac{r}{52r_w}\right)v^m = p^m. \qquad (17)$$

If the assumptions made here apply to every industry in the system then, in our usual notation, (17) leads to

$$(1+r)p^mA+m\left(\frac{r}{52r_w}\right)a = p^m. \qquad (18)$$

Relations (17) and (18) are the *exact* relations between money prices, the annual profit rate and the weekly profit rate; it is natural to ask, however, whether (17) is *better approximated* by

$$(1+r)(c^m+v^m) = p^m \qquad (19)$$

or by

$$(1+r)c^m+v^m = p^m, \qquad (20)$$

that is, by the assumption that *all* wages are paid at the beginning of the year or by the assumption that they are *all* paid at the end. Since a general analysis of what is only a simple example might seem somewhat over elaborate, Table III presents a few selected values of r_w and the corresponding values of r and of $(r/52r_w)$.[8]

Table III

r_w %	r %	$(r/52r_w)$
0.2	10.95	1.05
0.3	16.85	1.08
0.4	23.07	1.11

[8] Figures in the second and third columns have been rounded off.

It will be seen that $(r/52r_w)$ always lies between 1 and $(1+r)$; indeed in each row $(r/52r_w)$ is just a little less than $(1+\frac{1}{2}r)$. Since this result holds for all plausible values of r_w and r, it may be said that (19) and (20) are about equally (un-)acceptable, with (20) in fact having the slight advantage.

The above example is readily generalized to the case in which wages are paid at the end of n equal periods, the interest rate r_n being defined by $(1+r_n)^n \equiv (1+r)$. (17) and (18) still hold, provided only that $(r/52r_w)$ is replaced by (r/nr_n). It can then be shown that $1 < (r/nr_n) < (1+r)$, for r positive and n finite, and indeed that a reasonable approximation (for small r) is that $(r/nr_n) \doteq [1+\frac{1}{2}(r - r_n)]$.[9] Hence complete post-payment of wages gives a slightly better approximation to the exact result than does complete pre-payment.

It will be clear that the above type of analysis can be extended to cover the case in which produced means of production are not all paid for at the beginning of the production period.[10]

The wage rate and the rate of exploitation
A change in the real wage *rate*,[11] whether brought about by a change in real wages or by a change in hours of work, will cause an inverse change in the rate of exploitation, *provided that* no change in the method of production is brought about. It will be shown here, however, that if there is a choice of production methods, then a higher real wage rate may be associated with a lower or with a higher rate of exploitation, when the latter is defined and measured in the usual way.

Consider a simple capitalist economy in which the *net* product[12]

[9] Consider the relation $n \log(1+r_n) = \log(1+r)$, with each side expanded in a Taylor series.

[10] See both the final section of the present chapter and the final section of chapter 12 for further consideration of turnover problems.

[11] The real wage per unit of working time.

[12] Gross product *minus* the replacements of the used up produced means of production; net product thus includes wages here.

106

consists of just one commodity, which is the wage good. Each available combination of single product, circulating capital production methods – each 'technique' – has the very special property that the 'value composition of capital' is the same in each line of production; consequently, production prices are always strictly proportional to values. As is well-known, the inverse relation between the real wage rate, w, and the rate of profit, r, will therefore be linear for each 'technique'.[13] Figure II shows that relation for two techniques, I and II. Under the provisional assumption that these are the only two techniques available, it will be seen that if w < w* then capi-

Figure II

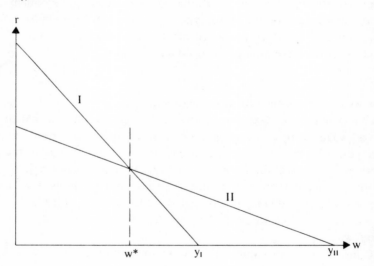

[13] *Cf.*, P. A. Samuelson, 'Parable and Realism in Capital Theory: The Surrogate Production Function', *Review of Economic Studies*, 1962 and P. Garegnani, 'Heterogeneous Capital, the Production Function and the Theory of Distribution', *ibid*, 1970. If prices of production are strictly proportional to values for every alternative technique then a 'neo-classical aggregate production' exists. This does *not* mean, however, that Marx's theory of the profit rate (and prices of production) then becomes the 'aggregate' neo-classical one, for Marx takes the real wage as given, whilst the neo-classical theory takes 'capital per worker' as given.

talists will choose technique I, while if w* < w they will choose technique II.[14]

If technique I is in use, the rate of exploitation, e, will be given by

$$(1 + e)(wl_I) = 1, \tag{21}$$

where l_I is the labour-time embodied in each unit of the wage good. The net product per unit of labour-time, when technique I is in use, is shown in the figure as y_I and, of course,

$$y_I l_I = 1. \tag{22}$$

From (21) and (22),

$$(1 + e) = (y_I/w), \tag{23}$$

provided that technique I is in use. If technique II is used, then analogous reasoning shows that

$$(1 + e) = (y_{II}/w). \tag{24}$$

Consider now what e will be for each level of w between 0 and y_{II} in Figure II. For $0 \leqq w < w*$ technique I will be used and e will be given by (23), while for $w* < w \leqq y_{II}$ technique II will be used and e will be given by (24); at $w = w*$ both techniques may be in use and e will be indeterminate (within the limits set by $(y_1/w*)$ and $(y_{II}/w*)$). Since $y_{II} > y_I$, it follows that e, while falling as w rises for each given technique, will 'jump up' as w rises across the value w*, as is shown in Figure III. Thus on comparing the rates of exploitation corresponding to two real wages rates w_1 and w_2, where $w_1 < w*$ $< w_2$, either rate may be found to be the larger. It cannot be assumed that a higher real wage rate involves a lower rate of exploitation when there is a choice of production methods.

If there are many alternative techniques, each with the 'equal value composition' property, then Figure II is merely rather more complicated, remaining essentially the same. Figure III will then be modified to Figure IV, in which y_j is the real wage rate at which

---

[14] For a given wage rate, capitalists will adopt the technique giving the highest rate of profit.

108

Figure III

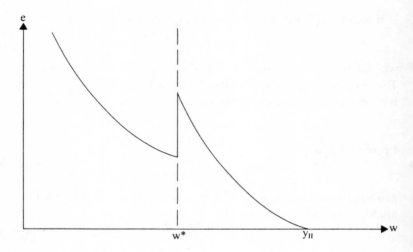

profits would be reduced to zero and each vertical dashed line occurs at a wage rate for which two alternative techniques are equally profitable. It will be seen that many different real wage rates can yield the same rate of exploitation.[15] (Figure IV will, in fact, apply in any system, no matter how many commodities enter the net product, provided that the *composition* of the wage bundle is independent of its level, w, and that no two individual techniques have wage-profit relations which intersect more than once. If such 'reswitching' does occur – a necessary condition for which is, of course, that not all techniques have the 'equal value composition' property – then e can 'jump down' at some values of w.)[16]

---

[15] Devotees of 'surrogate production functions' will recognize this result in the form that 'as one moves around the production function' the *share* of profits in the net product may rise, fall or remain constant, depending on the 'elasticity of substitution'.

[16] It may be of interest to note that the graph of (C/V) against w is very similar to that of e against w, as shown in Figures III and IV.

Figure IV

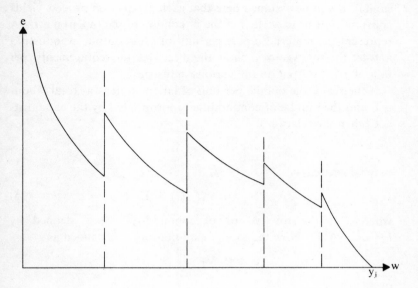

Thus in the presence of a choice of production methods, the real wage rate and the rate of exploitation are not necessarily inversely related. Since a higher wage and/or shorter hours can correspond to a higher rate of exploitation, as measured by $e \equiv (S/V)$ or, equivalently,

$$(1+e)(l \cdot w) = 1,$$

it would seem that this measure does not adequately capture the full intuitive meaning of the concept of exploitation.[17]

A role for value magnitudes?
Consider a simple capitalist economy in which n commodities are

[17] As was pointed out to me by Dott. Neri Salvadori.

produced by n single-product industries, using only circulating capital: it will be assumed here that each production process yields constant returns to scale. Let the jth column of the (n × n) matrix A represent the material inputs per unit of gross output in industry j and let the row vector a show the direct labour requirements, per unit of gross output, in the various industries.

If the real wage bundle per unit of labour-time is w, total labour is L and the bundle of commodities appropriated by the capitalists is C, then the relation

$$V + S = L$$

may be written as

$$(l \cdot w) L + (l \cdot C) = L, \tag{25}$$

where l is the row vector of commodity values, defined by $l = a(I - A)^{-1}$. Now the rate of exploitation, e, is defined as

$$e \equiv (S/V)$$

or

$$e \equiv [(l \cdot C)/(l \cdot w)L], \tag{26}$$

so that, using (26), one may rewrite (25) as

$$l \cdot C = \left(\frac{e}{1+e}\right)L. \tag{27}$$

Relation (27) shows that the *physical bundle* of commodities appropriated by the capitalists is constrained, for any given L, by the value magnitudes l and e. The 'role' of the value magnitudes is, so to speak, to determine the possible '*physical* forms' of the capitalists' total profit; yet as has been seen repeatedly above, those value magnitudes play no role in determining the *rate of profit*, which is the manifestation of the 'surplus' most characteristic of – specific to – the capitalist form of society. Thus value magnitudes are relevant to the determination of the physical form of the surplus – something which is not specific to capitalism – and irrelevant to the determination of the rate of profit – the specific feature of capitalism.

It is, of course, the case that one does not *need* to refer explicitly to the value magnitudes, even for the purpose of discussing the physical form of the surplus. Relation (25) can be written as

$$a(I - A)^{-1} \cdot C = [1 - a(I - A)^{-1}w]L,$$

which shows directly, in terms of production conditions and the real wage bundle, the possible physical surplus bundles, C, for any given L. Anything that can be expressed in terms of value magnitudes can be expressed without them, since they are only derivates of the more fundamental physical production conditions and real wages. These latter can, of course, also be used to show how the social allocation of labour-time between industries is determined.[18] If X is the column vector of commodity gross outputs, then

$$X = AX + wL + C$$

and

$$L = a \cdot X;$$

hence

$$X = AX + (w \cdot a)X + C$$

or

$$X = [I - A - (w \cdot a)]^{-1}C. \tag{28}$$

Relation (28) shows how the pattern of gross outputs, X, depends on the conditions of production, A and a, on the real wage bundle, w, and on the level and composition of the physical surplus, C. Since total labour-time in industry j is equal to a_jX_j,[19] (28) also shows (implicitly) how the social allocation of labour is determined by A, a, w and C. No reference to any value magnitude is necessary for

---

[18] No account is taken here of the choice between *alternative* production methods: the determination of the social allocation of labour will be discussed in a far more general context in chapter 13.

[19] Where a_j is the jth component of a.

that determination.[20]

Pure circulation

It is sometimes thought useful to distinguish between productive activities, in a capitalist economy, and those activities concerned with 'pure circulation' processes. This distinction will be pursued briefly in the present section, albeit in a very simple way which should, nevertheless, suffice to indicate the kind of analysis that is required.

Suppose first that each productive activity, using only circulating capital and producing no joint products, takes one year, which is also the time taken for the circulation of commodities.[21] It will be assumed, for simplicity, that *all* commodities used in the process of production or used as inputs in the circulation process – pens, paper, telephones, etc. – are purchased *after* passing through the circulation process; to allow for the fact that, say, seed corn is not so acquired would merely complicate the analysis, while adding little. If the gross output of each commodity is unity, if wages are paid at the end of the year and if P^m and p^m are the money price vectors of commodities after and before circulation, respectively, then we have, for the productive sector, the relation.

$$(1+\mathrm{r})P^m\mathrm{A}+\mathrm{m}a = p^m, \qquad (29)$$

where r, A, m and *a* are to be interpreted as usual. Note that, in (29),

[20] It may be of interest to note here that quantities of embodied labour-time would not be of significance in the planning of a *growing* socialist economy. In a growing economy, account must be taken not merely of the total labour-time required to produce a commodity but also of the 'time-pattern' of the expenditure of that total. (At a formal level, the point involved here is completely analogous to the importance of the 'time-pattern' of labour expenditures for the determination of the profit rate in a capitalist economy – *cf.*, chapter 5, above.) The full physical data, concerning production methods and planned real consumption, etc. bundles, would be required for the adequate planning of a growing economy – which is not to say that nothing else would be needed!

[21] A shorter circulation period will be considered below.

the productive sector sells commodities to the circulation sector at prices p^m, but purchases from it at prices P^m. The corresponding relation for the circulation sector is

$$(1+r)(p^m + P^m A^c) + ma^c = P^m, \tag{30}$$

where A^c is the matrix of commodity inputs used up in the circulation process – waste paper baskets, etc. – and a^c is the vector of labour-times devoted to circulation. It is implicit in (30) that wages are paid *ex post*, that waste paper baskets and so on are purchased at the *post* circulation prices, P^m, and that there is a distinct circulation activity for each commodity: only the last of these assumptions would be difficult to change.[22]

Now it follows from (29) and (30) that the post circulation prices are given by

$$P^m = m[(1+r)a + a^c][I - (1+r)A^c - (1+r)^2 A]^{-1}. \tag{31}$$

Thus if the real wage bundle per unit of labour-time is w then, since $m = P^m \cdot w$ if workers do not save, it follows that

$$[(1+r)a + a^c][I - (1+r)A^c - (1+r)^2 A]^{-1}w = 1. \tag{32}$$

By contrast, if the circulation activities were unnecessary, so that (29) would have p^m on both sides, then r would be determined by

$$a[I - (1+r)A]^{-1}w = 1. \tag{33}$$

It is not difficult to see that the rate of profit determined by (32) is *lower* than that yielded by (33); the presence of circulation activities makes the rate of profit lower than it would be were they unnecessary.[23]

Circulation in effect lowers the profit rate in two different ways: first by extending the total turnover time of commodities and second

[22] Even this assumption becomes unnecessary when joint production activities are allowed for, as in chapters 12 and 13.

[23] If such activities *were* unnecessary, in the capitalist economy considered, then the drive to maximize the rate of profit would bring about their elimination.

by using up material inputs and labour-time. To see the influence of the mere extension of turnover time, suppose that produced commodities had to wait a year before being sold, even though nothing whatever was 'done' in that circulation period. In (32), A^c and a^c would then both be null, so that

$$(1 + r)a[I - (1 + r)^2 A]^{-1} w = 1. \tag{34}$$

Relation (34) determines a lower value of r than does (33), even though no materials or labour-time are used in circulation, simply on account of the increase in total turnover time. On the other hand, the r yielded by (32) is even lower than that given by (34), so that the using up of materials and labour-time in circulation does cause a reduction in r, additional to that caused by the extension of the turnover time.

While it is certainly true that the difference between the profit rates determined by (32) and (33) is *related to* the fact that in the economy represented by (32) labour is being performed in the circulation sector itself and in the production sector to produce the material inputs and the real wage goods absorbed by the circulation sector – this not being so in the economy represented by (33) – it will be clear that the difference in profit rates cannot be adequately *explained in terms of* any simple difference between aggregate labour-times. An adequate proximate explanation can, however, be provided using a full physical specification of the real wage and of the conditions of production and circulation.

The assumption, used above, of equal periods of production and circulation may well exaggerate the increase in turnover time resulting from circulation activities. Suppose instead, then, that all production activities take one year, with wages being paid weekly, at the end of the week (as assumed earlier in this chapter) and that each circulation activity takes just one week, wages again being paid at the end of the week. Modifying our previous notation, it can be shown that (32) must be modified to

$$\left[(1 + r_w)\left(\frac{r}{52r_w}\right)a + a^c\right][I - (1 + r_w)(1 + r)A - (1 + r_w)A^c]^{-1} w = 1,$$

$$\tag{35}$$

where $(1+r_w)^{52} \equiv (1+r)$ and gross output of each commodity is one unit *per week*, it being assumed that a year-long production activity is started every week for each commodity, so that A, a, A^c, a^c now refer to the inputs used in the production, or circulation, of *one week's* output. Relation (35) shows the effect on the annual rate of profit, r, of both the addition of a one week circulation period to total turnover time and the use of materials and labour in the circulation sector. It will be clear that more complex combinations of production and circulation periods could be examined, by the same methods of analysis as used here for a very simple case, and that such analysis will involve no reference to any value magnitudes. It will show that the rate of profit can be determined only in terms of the full, physical details of production and circulation activities and of the real wage.

9

A Falling Rate of Profit?

Marx's discussion of the 'tendency of the rate of profit to fall' apparently continues to exert a considerable fascination, even though it is well-established that no definite conclusions may be drawn from that discussion. The first section of the present chapter is devoted to an examination of the mutual consistency of certain of Marx's expectations concerning trends over time of a number of variables,[1] no attempt being made to question the plausibility of those expectations. The second section, by contrast, does raise such questions, and provides some critical comments on familiar arguments. In the third section, the issue is considered within the framework of analysis adopted throughout this book.

I. The Mutual Consistency of Marx's Expectations

In his essay 'The Falling Rate of Profit', Meek considers the two principal objections that have been levelled against Marx's well-

---

[1] It may be of interest to note here the following two passages from *Theories of Surplus Value* (Part II, London, 1969, p. 453 and Part III, London, 1972, pp. 364–5, respectively):

'Incidentally, when speaking of the law of the *falling rate of profit* in the course of the development of capitalist production, we mean by profit, the total sum of surplus-value which is seized in the first place by [the] industrial capitalist, [irrespective of] how he may have to share this later with the money-lending capitalist (in the form of interest) and the landlord (in the form of rent).'

known discussion of 'The Law of the Tendency of the Rate of Profit to Fall' in *Capital*, volume III, part III.[2] The first, that a rising composition of capital will generally be associated with rising productivity (falling values) and will thus tend to raise the rate of exploitation, Meek, following Rosdolsky,[3] considers not to be an objection at all, on the grounds that Marx took adequate account of this association. The second objection, that technical progress may not raise the value composition of capital, is, Meek suggests, 'rather more justified'. Meek concludes: 'The main criticism which can properly be made of Marx's treatment of the problem is that nowhere does he precisely define the conditions under which the rate of profit will fall with a rising organic composition of capital, if we assume that this rising organic composition is associated with the lowering of the value of elements not only of variable but also of constant capital.'[4]

The purpose of this section is to provide a highly abstract analysis which does allow for the cheapening of the elements of both variable and constant capital. It will be shown that Marx's normal assumptions do entail a rising value composition of capital, despite the cheapening of the constant capital, and conditions will be derived under which a rising rate of surplus value, a rising value composition of capital and a falling rate of profit are mutually consistent. The argument is conducted both in terms of the variables normally used in Marxist theory and in terms of the observable variables of production conditions and the real wage, a subordinate objective being to emphasize the relations between the two sets of variables. We

---

'For us, however, the main thing is: does this fact [the rise in (C/V) – I.S.] explain the decline in the rate of profit? (A decline, incidentally, which is far smaller than it is said to be.)'

[2] R. L. Meek, 'The Falling Rate of Profit', in *Economics and Ideology and Other Essays*, London, 1967. An earlier version appeared in *Science and Society*, 1960.

[3] R. Rosdolsky, 'Zur Neuren Kritik des Marxschen Gesetzes der fallenden Profitrate', *Kyklos*, 1956.

[4] Meek, *op. cit.*, p. 136.

assume throughout a circulating-capital, input-output system in which every sector has the same value composition of capital;[5] it will be clear that strong simplifications are being made but at least they are simplifications of a type sometimes made by Marx himself.

The framework

Consider a circulating capital system with unchanging production conditions (A, a) in our usual notation. If l_i be defined as the total amount of labour used, both directly and indirectly, in the production of one unit of commodity i, (as the value of commodity i) then

$$l = lA + a. \tag{1}$$

Using c, v and s to represent the vectors of constant capital, variable capital and surplus value per unit of output respectively, we have that

$$c = lA \qquad \text{and} \qquad v + s = a$$

so that (1) could be rewritten as

$$l = c + v + s.$$

It is assumed that the rate of exploitation, or rate of surplus value, e, is the same in every sector so that, by definition,

$$s = ev$$

and thus

$$(1 + e)v = a. \tag{2}$$

If the value composition of capital is the same in every sector, then the vector c must be proportional to the vector v and hence, from (2), to the vector a. It can be shown that the factor of proportionality is given by

$$Rc = a \tag{3}$$

[5] It follows from this that any reader unfamiliar with matrices and vectors will lose little by interpreting all variables as scalars.

where R is the maximum possible rate of profit in the system, which is determined entirely by A. (It is assumed, for simplicity, that A is irreducible.) The result that the maximum rate of profit, R, is equal to the ratio of current labour to the labour embodied in the means of production is, of course, to be expected in the equal value composition of capital case, since prices are here proportional to values. From (2) and (3) we have that

$$Rc = (1+e)v$$

so that in every sector, and hence overall, the value composition of capital is given by

$$\left(\frac{c}{v}\right) = \left(\frac{1+e}{R}\right). \tag{4}$$

It will be noted that while 'R' is a 'technological' variable, depending only on A, 'e' is not, so that it would be quite wrong to think of the value composition of capital as merely a description of the conditions of production.[6]

On substituting from (4) into Marx's formula for the rate of profit,

$$r = \left[\frac{e}{1+(c/v)}\right]$$

we obtain

$$r = \left(\frac{eR}{1+e+R}\right). \tag{5}$$

The real wage

Suppose that the real wage consists of w_i of the ith commodity per hour of labour where some w_i will be positive and some zero. (Marx, of course, normally worked in terms of a daily wage which

[6] It may be noted that the ratio $(c/v+s) = R^{-1}$ *is* a 'technological' variable, given normal working practices.

did not necessarily change as the length of the working day changed.) By definition, the value of one hour's labour power is $\Sigma_i w_i l_i$ and hence

$$v = (\Sigma_i w_i l_i)a. \tag{6}$$

Comparing (2) and (6) we see that

$$(1+e) = \left(\frac{1}{\Sigma_i w_i l_i}\right). \tag{7}$$

Noticing from (1) and (3) that

$$l = \left(\frac{1+R}{R}\right) a$$

and introducing the notation

$$\lambda \equiv \lambda^{PF}(A) = \left(\frac{1}{1+R}\right) \tag{8}$$

we can rewrite (7) as

$$(1+e) = \left[\frac{1-\lambda}{\Sigma_i w_i a_i}\right]. \tag{9}$$

$\lambda \equiv \lambda^{PF}(A)$, the Perron–Frobenius root of the matrix A, is a useful summary variable since it is an increasing function of every element of the input-output matrix A; variations in λ thus indicate the extent to which the overall use of produced inputs is increasing or decreasing, relative to gross output.

It may be noted that

$$\lambda = \left(\frac{c}{c+v+s}\right),$$

i.e. the ratio of the value of constant capital to the value of gross output and that

$$1-\lambda = \left(\frac{v+s}{c+v+s}\right),$$

i.e. the ratio of the value of net output to the value of gross output. It will also prove useful to define W as

$$W = \Sigma w_i a_i = \left(\frac{v}{c+v+s}\right),$$

i.e. the ratio of the value of labour power, or variable capital, to the value of gross output. It is thus easy to translate later results in terms of λ and W, which directly express the observable variables of production conditions and the real wage, into results in terms of the shares of constant capital, variable capital and surplus value in total value. By using (8) and (9) our expressions for (c/v) and r can be reformulated in terms of A, a and w. Drawing our results together now, for convenience, we have:

$$(1+e) = \left(\frac{1-\lambda}{W}\right) \tag{10}$$

$$\left(\frac{c}{v}\right) = \left(\frac{1+e}{R}\right) = \left(\frac{\lambda}{W}\right) \tag{11}$$

$$(1+r) = \frac{(1+e)(1+R)}{1+e+R} = \left(\frac{1}{\lambda+W}\right) \tag{12}$$

Note that the right-hand side of each of (10), (11) and (12) is expressed directly in terms of A, a and w. (10), (11) and (12) thus show how three central ratios of Marxist economic theory (the rate of surplus value, the value composition of capital and the rate of profit) are related to observable variables. Consider now a sequence of periods such that within any period conditions of production and the real wage are constant but between periods production conditions change, either because social conditions change, or because new technical processes become available, or because a change in the real wage alters the relative profitabilities of existing production methods, or because old commodities cease to be produced and/or new commodities come into production. In each period the value composition of capital is the same in every sector and the periods are sufficiently long that toward the end of any period we need not be concerned at the 'undated' nature of equation (1); this last assumption is, of course, a rather delicate one! Bearing in mind that equations (10), (11) and (12) take account of the cheapening of *all* elements of *both* constant and variable capital, how might the end of period rate of profit be expected to move?

A falling rate of profit?

Marx makes a number of statements in *Capital*, vol. III, which entail that the maximum possible rate of profit, R, will fall through time. For example, in chapter 13 he writes of 'the individual commodity' that 'the portion of its value in which newly added labour is material- ised decreases in relation to the portion of its value which represents raw and auxiliary material, and the wear and tear of fixed capital'[7] and an equally explicit statement to the same effect appears in vol. III, chapter 15, section 4. That such statements entail a falling R may be seen from (3).

The assumption of a falling *maximum* rate of profit, R, did not, for Marx, guarantee a falling *actual* rate of profit, r, since Marx also assumed that the rate of surplus value, e, would tend to rise through time.[8] But the two assumptions of a falling R and a rising e do guarantee that the value composition of capital will tend to rise, as can be seen from (11). Thus given his normal assumptions about technological development and the distribution of value-added between workers and capitalists, Marx was perfectly entitled, indeed he was obliged, to assume a rising value composition of capital, despite the cheapening of the elements of constant capital.

Since the value composition of capital itself depends on the rate of surplus value, see (11), it is potentially confusing to think of the rate of profit as the rate of surplus value divided by one plus the value composition of capital: it would seem better to relate r to R and e as is done in (12). It is then easy to show from (8) and (12) that

[7] Moscow, 1966, p. 227.

[8] *Cf.*, Meek, *op. cit.*, Rosdolsky, *op. cit.*, and P. M. Sweezy, *The Theory of Capitalist Development*, London, 1962, p. 101.

r will fall if, and only if,

$$\left(\frac{c}{v}\right)\left(\frac{\Delta\lambda}{\lambda}\right) > \left(\frac{\Delta e}{e + \Delta e}\right), \tag{13}$$

where $\Delta\lambda$ and Δe, the period to period changes in λ and e respectively, are both positive. While there seems to be no reason to assert that (13) *must* hold, it should be noted that with a falling R and a rising e, (c/v) will be rising so that (13) becomes ever easier to satisfy in the sense that an ever smaller percentage rise in λ can 'offset' a given percentage rise in e. The suggestions of Meek and Dickinson[9] that r might rise at first and subsequently fall are clearly consistent with this result, as is Meek's further suggestion that the 'downturn' in r will be further off in time, the lower are the initial value composition and rate of exploitation.

Turning now to our more explicit formulations for e, (c/v) and r in terms of production conditions and the real wage, an obvious question to ask is what time paths of production conditions and real wages are consistent with the simultaneous satisfaction of Marx's expectations of a rising e, a rising (c/v) and a falling r? It is easy to show that the necessary and sufficient conditions for this simultaneous satisfaction are given by

$$\left(\frac{c}{v}\right)\left(\frac{\Delta\lambda}{\lambda}\right) > \left(\frac{\Delta W}{W}\right) > \frac{1}{R}\left(\frac{\Delta\lambda}{\lambda}\right) \tag{14}$$

where $\Delta\lambda$ and ΔW, the period to period *increase* in λ and *decrease* in W respectively, are both positive. (It should be noted, of course, that provided some of the a_i associated with positive w_i are decreasing, a falling W does not entail a falling real wage.) With λ increasing and W decreasing, (c/v) will necessarily increase; the left-hand inequality in (14) gives the condition for a falling r and the right-hand one that for a rising e. It will be noticed that an ever smaller percentage increase in λ is sufficient to 'offset' a given percentage fall in W and thus lower the rate of profit but that, on the other hand, an ever

[9] Meek, *op. cit.*, and H. D. Dickinson, 'The Falling Rate of Profit in Marxian Economics', *Review of Economic Studies*, 1956–7.

smaller percentage rise in λ is sufficient to 'offset' a given percentage fall in W and thus to stop the rate of exploitation from rising.

The preceding paragraph would seem, in the context of a simple economy and in a purely formal way, to provide the conditions that Meek finds lacking in Marx.

The results obtained above are, of course, highly formal; we have not allowed for the influence of differing turnover periods of capital or differences in value composition between sectors (thus pushing out of sight the question of the relative rates of productivity increase in capital goods and wage goods industries) and have not even raised the question whether the formal conditions derived are likely to be satisfied empirically. Subject to these qualifications, it has been shown that Marx's assumption of a falling R and a rising e does guarantee that (c/v) will rise, even though the elements of constant capital are becoming cheaper, and that a rising e and rising (c/v) can, under the stated conditions, combine to yield a falling rate of profit.

II. Some Critical Remarks

It has been shown above that there is no internal inconsistency involved in asserting that, over time, the rate of exploitation and the value composition of capital increase, while both the maximum rate of profit and the actual rate of profit fall. That the four propositions in question are mutually *consistent*, however, does not mean that any one of them is factually correct. Nor does it mean that if the first three should, indeed, be correct then the truth of the fourth proposition follows.

Marx repeatedly *asserted* that the value composition of capital rises over time in capitalist economies.[10] This assertion occurs so frequently in Marx's writings and is so well-known that it is easy to forget that Marx *did not know* whether it was true or false. He could not have known, for the simple reason that the relevant information

---

[10] See the appendix to this chapter for references.

was just not available to him. The ratio (C/V) is the ratio of the labour embodied in the means of production to the labour embodied in the wage goods obtained by the workers. While this ratio is calculable *in principle*, the fact is that it never has been calculated, either in Marx's time or since, and that such a calculation would, in practice, be very difficult to carry out. Neither Marx nor anyone else has ever known the magnitude of (C/V) for a single economy, even at one point of time, let alone known its trend over time. This fact must be respected and insisted on, no matter how often writers may assert that the value composition of capital rises through time in capitalist economies.

What Marx did know was that, in the early period of British capitalism, the 'mass' of means of production per worker – in some ill-defined sense – had increased dramatically. He also had a certain amount of statistical information relating to the money values of some produced means of production. Yet it is clear that no inference can be drawn from the increasing 'mass' of means of production per worker (however defined) concerning changes in (C/V). Nor may movements in the latter be deduced even from good, complete statistics referring to money aggregates – and Marx had only very incomplete statistics – since it cannot be known *a priori* that value ratios and money ratios will move in the same direction. Marx's assertion that (C/V) increases may, of course, have been correct but he did not know it to be so and nor do we.

Similar remarks can and should be made concerning the maximum rate of profit and the rate of exploitation. Marx did not know how the former was changing over time. With respect to the rate of exploitation, while it is again true that Marx did not *know* how it was moving (due to lack of the relevant data), it can be said that it was perhaps plausible for him to assume it to be rising. If the real wage bundle were strictly constant over time while, due to technical progress, the labour embodied in each wage good were falling, then the rate of exploitation would, of course, necessarily be rising. It was, perhaps, reasonable for Marx to infer that that rate was actually rising, on the grounds that the increase in real wages was not fast, while the rate of technical progress was. (It is no longer plausible to assume either direction of movement in the rate of exploitation and we certainly do not *know* how it is changing, over the long term, in the advanced capitalist countries in the 1950's, 60's and 70's.)

Turning to more recent discussions of the issue in hand, it may be noted first that increasing emphasis is being given to the idea that the central question is whether the maximum possible rate of profit is falling. Whether that emphasis be well-advised or not, it should be noted that it would be quite wrong to suggest that if the maximum rate of profit is falling, then the actual rate of profit *must* eventually fall: that would be a simple *non sequitur*. To illustrate the point, let $f(t)$ be any function of time, t, such that $f(o) = 1$, while $f(t)$ becomes ever smaller as t increases, approaching zero as t approaches infinity.[11] Denote the maximum rate of profit, the rate of exploitation and the value composition of capital, at time t, by R_t, e_t and $(C/V)_t$ respectively, where:

$$R_t = 0.1 + 0.4f(t) \tag{15}$$

$$e_t = \left[\frac{11 + 4f(t)}{9 + 76f(t)}\right] \tag{16}$$

$$(C/V)_t = \left(\frac{1 + e_t}{R_t}\right) = \left[\frac{200}{9 + 76f(t)}\right] \tag{17}$$

It will be seen that as t increases from zero to infinity, R_t falls from 50% to 10%, e_t increases from (15/85) to (11/9) and $(C/V)_t$ rises from (200/85) to (200/9). Yet the actual rate of profit, according to Marx's formula, is given by

$$r_t = \left[\frac{e_t}{1 + (C/V)_t}\right] = \frac{1}{19}$$

for all t.

Thus while the maximum rate of profit always falls – and e and (C/V) always rise – the actual rate of profit is perfectly constant at

---

[11] E.g., $f(t) \equiv a^t$, where $0 < a < 1$.

just over $5\frac{1}{4}\%$. Indeed, if e_t rose ever so slightly faster than is stated by (16), while R_t and $(C/V)_t$ moved as stated by (15) and (17), then r_t would always be *rising* over time, despite the unending fall in R_t.[12] (It need hardly be said that this example has only the 'negative' function of a counter-example; it is not supposed to be 'realistic'.)

A second feature of recent discussions, which may merit a brief comment, relates to the interaction of individual capitalist decisions and their overall effect. For any given technique of production there is an inverse relation between the real wage rate and the rate of profit. A similar inverse relation therefore obtains even when there are alternative production methods between which the capitalists choose. Thus, in Figure I, the curve AB depicts the inverse relation between the real wage rate, w, and the rate of profit, r, when Tech-

Figure I

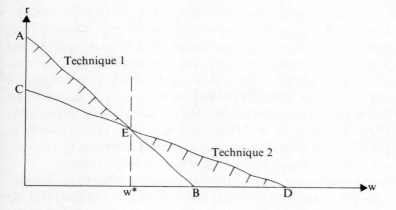

nique 1 is used; the curve CD shows the corresponding relation for Technique 2. Since capitalists will choose the technique yielding the

[12] In other words, the unending decrease of R_t must eventually lead to a decrease in r_t *only if* R_t tends to *zero* as t tends to infinity.

highest attainable rate of profit at any given real wage rate, it may be seen that if the wage should be below w* then Technique 1 will be chosen, while if it should be greater than w*, Technique 2 will be chosen.[13] Thus the hatched curve AED is the *effective* relation between r and w in this economy.[14] It will be clear that the existence of more alternative techniques would not lead to any change in the nature of Figure I, merely making it rather more complicated.

Suppose now that technical progress occurs, for whatever reason. Whether it be regarded as involving 'improvements' in one or more existing techniques or as involving the creation of one or more essentially new techniques, that progress will be economically relevant only if it causes at least some part of the frontier AED to move 'outwards from the origin', so that higher rates of profit now correspond to at least some given real wage rates. The 'new' frontier will still be downward sloping. It is thus impossible for the rate of profit *after* the technical advance to be less than that *before* the advance, unless the real wage-rate has risen. With a given real wage, technical progress can only raise the rate of profit, never lower it.

Now some writers have been tempted to confuse this straight-forward argument by asserting (correctly) that decentralized, individual decisions need not always lead, in aggregate, to the achievement of the commonly pursued objective and by then inferring (incorrectly) that while each individual capitalist will respond to new technical possibilities by seeking to maximize his rate of profit, the overall effect can be to lower the new, uniform rate of profit, even at an unchanged real wage rate. This 'argument' is just silly. For unless the previously adopted technique is no longer available, it is being asserted that, after the change, capitalists are no longer maximizing the rate of profit attainable with the given wage! Even if a new invention should lead many capitalists mistakenly to adopt it, as soon as it is found to be less profitable than the previously

---

[13] If w = w* then either or both may be chosen.

[14] It would, of course, be possible to allow for changes in hours and intensity of work – *cf.*, chapter 6 – but such changes are perhaps less important in a long-period than in a short-period context.

used technique, all capitalists will revert to the latter. With a given real wage, the rate of profit can be lowered only by technical *regress*, never by technical progress.

Since technical knowledge has seldom, if ever, been lost *beyond recovery* within the capitalist era,[15] technical regress can result only from worsening conditions in the production of food, raw materials, fuels, minerals, etc. With a given real wage, a falling rate of profit can therefore result only from the increasing niggardliness of nature, the very factor which Marx was so anxious *not* to rely on in his theory of the tendency of the profit rate to fall![16]

III. The Alternative Framework

The above discussion has been conducted without reference to the fact that, as was seen in chapters 3, 4, 5 and 8, Marx's formula for the rate of profit is, in general, invalid. Whether or not the main issues involved can be brought out using Marx's incorrect formula,[17] it is clearly desirable to examine them in the context of a correct formulation.

It would obviously be inappropriate to consider the question of the movement of the rate of profit over time in an analysis ignoring fixed capital, such as that presented in previous chapters. It will be shown in chapter 12, however, that whether fixed capital is used or

[15] It is not relevant – though it is interesting – to ask whether pre-capitalist technical knowledge has been lost beyond recall.

[16] Of course, Marx *did* at one point appeal to precisely this factor, in order to 'show' that cheapening of the raw material, etc., components of constant capital would not decisively counteract the alleged tendency of the value composition of capital to rise – *cf.*, *Theories of Surplus Value*, Part III, London, 1972, p. 368. For an interesting discussion of this point and, more generally, of Marx on technical progress, see B. Schefold, 'Different Forms Of Technical Progress', *Economic Journal*, 1976.

[17] See, for example, G. Hodgson, 'The Theory of the Falling Rate of Profit', *New Left Review*, no. 84, 1974, for a survey of the traditional arguments which 'accept' this formula as the basis of discussion. In his paper 'Marx's Falling Rate of Profit: A Dialectical View', *Canadian Journal of Economics*, 1976, M. Lebowitz, while still using Marx's formula, significantly extends the range of the traditional debate to include the discussion of 'realization' problems.

not, the rate of profit, r, in a given period is determined by the relation

$$(1 + r)l(I - rH)^{-1}w = 1 \qquad (18)$$

where l and w are the row vector of labour values and the column vector showing the real wage bundle per unit of labour, respectively.[18] The square matrix H shows, as will be explained in greater detail in chapter 12, the physical capital stocks required, whether directly or indirectly, for the production of the various commodities. The rate of exploitation, e, is, of course, defined by

$$(1 + e)(l \cdot w) \equiv 1. \qquad (19)$$

Before examining the movement of the rate of profit, it may be helpful to note that, appearances notwithstanding, (18) and (19) are closely related to the simple formula (12), [reproduced here for convenience;

$$(1 + r) = \frac{(1 + e)(1 + R)}{1 + e + R} \qquad (12)]$$

in the sense that (18) and (19) collapse to (12) in certain special cases. Suppose first that there is only one commodity, so that l, H and w are all scalars; since $R \cdot H = 1$, relation (12) can now be deduced immediately from (18) and (19). *Somewhat* more generally, in the equal composition of capital case – in which $l = R/H$ – or in the case of w being a characteristic vector of $H - RHw = w - (18)$ and (19) again imply (12). While this relationship between (12), (18) and (19) may serve to make (18) seem less unfamiliar, it must be remembered that (12) holds *only* in very special cases; (18) is far more generally valid.

What can be said then about the movement of the rate of profit, on the basis of relation (18)? It must be noted first that the changes over time in l, H and w do not, of course, consist merely of changes in magnitudes. Over time, the list of commodities produced in an

---

[18] It is assumed in (18) that wages are paid in advance; if they are paid *ex post*, then (18) still holds provided that the initial term $(1 + r)$ is suppressed.

economy will change, new commodities being added and, sometimes, 'old' commodities disappearing from the list. This fact alone
is sufficient to make it unlikely that any *a priori* expectation about
the movement of r will be well-founded.

If the set of commodities produced *is* the same in two different
periods, so that *l*, H and *w* differ (as between those periods) only in
magnitude, then in contemporary, advanced capitalist economies
one must expect that *w* will be as great or greater (in each of its
elements) in the later period than in the earlier one.[19] Other things
equal, this would reduce the rate of profit as between the two periods
but, of course, both *l* and H will also change, in general. The general
advance of labour productivity will be manifested by the fact that
most elements of *l* will probably be lower in the later period. It must,
however, be remembered in this connection that worsening conditions of production of food, raw materials, etc., *might* lead some
elements of *l* actually to increase over time.[20] It would seem that
little can be said about the likely changes in the elements of H.[21]
(One cannot say, it must be remembered, that they will tend to rise
because 'more and more' means of production are used in production, since most such changes involve qualitative changes in the
nature of the produced means of production, so that the pre- and
post-change H matrices cannot be compared in any simple, unambiguous way, contrary to the assumption made in this paragraph.)

---

[19] Real wages do sometimes fall over *short* periods, of course, but the discussion is not about short period changes.

[20] It is not being asserted that this is in fact known to happen.

[21] To compare the force of (18) and (19) with Marx's argument, suppose
(arbitrarily) that *w* grows steadily, and *l* falls steadily, at the positive rate g,
so that $w_t = w_0(1+g)^t$ and $l_t = l_0(1+g)^{-t}$. It follows at once from (19) that
the rate of exploitation, e_t, will be constant over time. Relation (18) may now
be written as

$$(1+r_t)l_0(I - r_tH_t)^{-1}w_0 = 1, \qquad (18')$$

since the factors $(1+g)^t$ and $(1+g)^{-t}$ cancel out. Asserting that $\lambda^{PF}(H_t) = R_t^{-1}$
tends to rise, i.e., R_t tends to fall, is the closest one can approach to Marx's
assertions about the rising composition of capital. Yet a falling R_t in (18') does
not guarantee a falling r_t, even though e_t is constant.

It can only be concluded that there are probably some forces a
work tending to increase r and some tending to decrease r over time
There appears to be no rational basis for expecting one tendency t
prevail rather than the other, over any given period, nor for expect
ing the relative strengths of the forces for the increase and those fo
the decrease of r to be unchanging.[22]

Appendix. The Composition of Capital

In discussion of Marx's work, the terms 'organic composition o
capital' and 'value composition of capital' are often used inter
changeably but Marx expressly distinguished between them.

'The composition of capital is to be understood in a twofold sense
As value, it is determined by the proportion in which it is divided
into constant capital, or the value of the means of production, and
variable capital, or the value of labour-power, the sum total o
wages. As material, as it functions in the process of production, all
capital is divided into means of production and living labour-power
This latter composition is determined by the relation between the
mass of the means of production employed on the one hand, and the
mass of labour necessary for their employment on the other. I call
the former the value-composition, the latter the technical composi-

[22] It might be said that this was precisely Marx's own conclusion, for did he
not discuss both a tendency for r to fall and counteracting influences? As Fine
and Harris put it (*op. cit.*, pp. 162–3), 'A more accurate name for Marx's
theory would be "the law of the tendency of the rate of profit to fall *and* of
the tendency for counteracting influences to operate".' Yet however the matter
is presented, there is a difference between asserting a tendency, which is probably counteracted, and asserting that there are forces acting in each direction,
there being no basis for regarding the forces in either direction as being the
more fundamental. Marx's presentation does convey a presumption that one
set of forces *is* the more fundamental and it is important to be clear that no
such presumption has ever been adequately established, by Marx or by
anyone else. (That apparent presumption may, of course, have been merely
an unfortunate consequence of Marx's concern to argue, against Ricardo,
that a falling rate of profit theory did not have to be based on the limiting role
of agricultural land; it was certainly that concern which led Marx so to emphasize the alleged rise in the composition of capital.)

tion of capital. There is a close correlation between the two. To express this, I call the value-composition of capital, in so far as it is determined by its technical composition and mirrors the changes in the latter, the organic composition of capital. Wherever I refer to the composition of capital, without further qualification, its organic composition is always understood.'

And again:

'The value composition of capital, inasmuch as it is determined by, and reflects, its technical composition, is called the *organic* composition of capital.'[23]

The meaning of 'value composition' is clear enough: it is the ratio of the two value quantities C and V. It is clear, too, from the first quoted passage, that the 'technical composition' refers to the 'proportion' between the physically specified means of production and the number of workers who operate and use them. Less clear, though, is how the technical composition can be measured (conceptually that is), since it refers to a bundle of quantities of heterogeneous commodities. If it is to be taken as just a vector of heterogeneous quantities, which is perhaps the most obvious interpretation, then it must be recognized that it will generally not be possible to say that the technical composition is greater (or smaller) at one point in time than at another, for the two sets of commodities involved will generally be qualitatively different. (A coal miner in 1970 uses both more electricity and fewer pit ponies than did a coal miner in 1870 – the *technical* composition is thus neither greater nor smaller in 1970 than in 1870.) If some other 'measure' is intended, what is it?

Still less transparent is the meaning of the 'organic composition', for it can hardly be said that Marx's definitions, involving the terms 'in so far as', 'mirrors', 'inasmuch as' and 'reflects', are models of precision. An interesting and plausible interpretation has, however,

[23] The first quotation is taken from *Capital*, vol. I, chapter 25, section 1 (Penguin/NLR edition, p. 762) and the second from *Capital*, vol. III, chapter 8 (Moscow, 1966 edition, pp. 145–6).

been given by Fine and Harris (*op. cit.*, p. 161). They suggest that 'the organic composition . . . is the same thing as the technical composition expressed in terms of values where the value[s] per unit of means of production and labour-power are the unit values which existed before the rise in technical composition'. At least in a situation in which a 'rise in technical composition' is unambiguous this interpretation (which is most straightforward in the presence of a constant real wage bundle) is clear and consistent with what Marx wrote.

Thus suppose that the wage bundle per worker is constant at w. At time t, let the vector of means of production be M_t, the number of workers be L_t and the vector of embodied labour quantities be l_t. Then the *value* composition is given by

$$(C/V)_t = \left[\frac{l_t \cdot M_t}{(l_t \cdot w)L_t} \right]$$

the *technical* composition (a vector) by

$$T_t = M_t \cdot L_t^{-1}$$

and the *organic* composition by

$$\text{O.C.C.}_t = \left[\frac{l_o \cdot M_t}{(l_o \cdot w)L_t} \right]$$

where time zero is taken as the pre-change point of comparison.

It may be noted that the organic composition, as here defined, is in effect an index number, for it follows immediately from the above that

$$\left(\frac{\text{O.C.C.}_t}{\text{O.C.C.}_o} \right) = \left(\frac{l_o \cdot T_t}{l_o \cdot T_o} \right).$$

The organic composition of capital is thus seen as a Laspeyres value-weighted index of means of production per worker. (Notice that it is not defined if T_t contains any commodities which did not exist at time zero.) It also follows from the above that

$$\text{O.C.C.}_t = \left(\frac{l_t \cdot w}{l_o \cdot w} \Big/ \frac{l_t \cdot T_t}{l_o \cdot T_t} \right) (C/V)_t.$$

The organic composition is thus equal to the value composition multiplied by the ratio of two indices of value changes, the one index using the wage bundle as weights and the other, a Paasche index, using the final period technical composition as weights. Obviously, then, O.C.C._t and $(C/V)_t$ move together provided that, speaking loosely, the values of wage goods and the values of means of production move 'in proportion' to one another.

Attention may now be turned to Marx's treatment of the (alleged) increases in the various compositions of capital. His discussions of the matter in *Capital*, vol. I (chapter 15, section vii, on machinery, and chapter 25, sections i, ii, on the 'General Law') and in *Capital*, vol. III (chapter 13, on the falling rate of profit) being so well-known and oft-cited, it may be of interest to consider rather his treatment of the question in *Theories of Surplus Value*, part III (chapter 23, on Cherbuliez).[24] A number of different formulations are to be found here.

On pages 364 and 367 Marx formulates the change in composition as involving an increase in constant capital relative to total living labour. This is expressed on p. 364 both by the assertion that $(C/C+V+S)$ increases as capital is accumulated and by the direct statement that $(C/V+S)$ increases; on p. 367 it is expressed as a fall in $(V+S/C)$ – obviously, all three formulations come to the same thing. On p. 366, however, a different assertion is found, namely that (C/V) increases. Again, on p. 365 the rising composition is expressed in terms of 'the decreasing number of workers relatively to the number and extent of the machinery employed'. Finally, the different formulations are fused in the following passage: 'It is

[24] All page references will be to the London, 1972 edition. This interesting chapter also includes the passages on the fall of the profit rate being far smaller than commonly thought and on the role of land in inhibiting the cheapening of constant capital, both cited above, in footnotes 1 and 16 respectively.

therefore self-evident or a tautological proposition that the increasing productivity of labour caused by machinery corresponds to increased value of the machinery relative to the amount of labour employed (consequently to the value of labour, the variable capital)' (pp. 366–7). Whether or not the proposition be 'tautological' – certainly the 'consequently' is inappropriate – Marx does here seem to regard all the 'compositions of capital' as increasing together, despite their different definitions.

It must be remarked, however, that the discussion of this appendix is of interest, if at all, only for its own sake: *neither* the value composition *nor* the organic composition is a significant concept for the analysis of capitalist economies. Only the technical composition, expressed as a vector of physically specified commodities, is of significance for such analysis – and it does not, of course, involve any reference whatever to any concept of embodied labour-time.

10

Fixed Capital

The role of fixed capital is clearly of the greatest importance in capitalist economies and it was no less central to Marx's analysis of them. Yet, with the one exception of a passing reference in the previous chapter, fixed capital has not so far been discussed in the present work. The analysis of fixed capital and of joint production will therefore be taken up in this[1] and the following three chapters.

Fixed capital and joint production are discussed together because the correct analysis of fixed capital requires that partially used up machines be treated as joint products. If a capitalist purchases some raw cotton, a new spinning machine and, say, one year's labour-power then, if all goes well from the capitalist's point of view he will possess, at the end of the year, both some saleable cotton thread and a one-year old spinning machine. After a second, similar year's operation he will possess some further vendible cotton yarn and a two-year old spinning machine; and so on until the machine is scrapped. Thus each year's operation, except the last, yields, in effect, two *joint products* – cotton thread and a 'one-year older' spinning machine. Hence the analysis of fixed capital is a (very important) special case of the analysis of joint production.[2] That old

---

[1] I should like to thank G. M. Hodgson for permitting me to draw, in this chapter, on our earlier joint work.

[2] The term '*pure* joint products' is used to denote joint products neither (or none) of which is an old machine, e.g., coke, coal, tar and town gas. Marx was well aware of the existence of pure joint products: see, e.g. *Capital*, vol. I,

machines not only can be but should be treated as joint products will emerge below.[3]

In this chapter two numerical examples will be used to show that, in the presence of fixed capital, the embodied labour-time values of commodities cannot be correctly calculated by adopting Marx's assumption of linear value depreciation of machinery; that the joint product approach can be used to calculate values; and that, when properly calculated, old machine values can be either negative or positive and, in the latter case, may even exceed the value of a new machine. This analysis provides yet another demonstration that correct, coherent value determinations *must* be based on the relevant, disaggregated physical data. 'Must', that is, if they are to be determined *at all*; the physical data referring to production conditions and real wages are entirely adequate to the (proximate) determination of the profit rate (and prices of production), no value magnitude being of the slightest relevance to that determination.

In the next chapter, chapter 11, a simple numerical example will be used to show that with *pure* joint products – and no fixed capital – Marx's additive value accounts can lead to the result that surplus value can be *negative* even when the rate of profit is positive. Chapters 12 and 13 will then present far more general analyses of fixed capital and joint product systems. It will, again, be found that no value magnitude is significant for the determination of the rate of profit (or prices of production) or indeed for that of the rate of accumulation and the social allocation of labour.

Marx's treatment of value depreciation

In *Capital*, Marx considered a number of different types of fixed capital, of different life spans and rates of depreciation. He even

---

p. 313, *Capital*, vol. III, chapter V, section IV and *Theories of Surplus Value*, part II, London, 1969, p. 486. For Marx's awareness that old machines may be treated as joint products, see the text below.

[3] This approach has been adopted by, for example, J. von Neumann (see chapter 13 below) and by P. Sraffa, *op. cit.*, Part II.

included a discussion of machines' having rising efficiency for certain periods of their lives, as well as the more frequent consideration of falling or constant efficiency. He was well aware of the complexity and heterogeneity of fixed capital in capitalist economies.

However, at least in one respect, he did not give general recognition to this at the theoretical level. When discussing the way in which a machine gradually loses its value over its life he assumed, in general, that the machine yields up its value in a constant, linear manner; so that the machine loses an equal amount of value for each year of its life. This conception of linear value depreciation is clearly evident from the following passage, which discusses depreciation in completely general terms:

'A proportion of the advanced capital-value becomes *fixed* in this form determined by the function of the instruments of labour in the process. In the performance of this function, and thus by the wear and tear of the instruments of labour, a part of their value passes on to the product, while the other remains fixed in the instruments of labour and thus in the process of production. The value fixed in this way decreases steadily until the instrument of labour is worn out, its value having been distributed during a shorter or longer period over a mass of products originating from a series of constant repeated labour-processes ... The longer an instrument lasts, the slower it wears out, the longer will its constant capital-value remain fixed in this use-form. But whatever may be its durability, the proportion in which it yields value is always inverse to the entire time it functions. If of two machines of equal value one wears out in five years and the other in ten, then the first yields twice as much value in the same time as the second.'[4]

Many similar passages could be quoted; for example the following one, which first presents the idea of linear depreciation and then, interestingly in view of the arguments developed below, suggests that linear depreciation is not always appropriate. for example when an

[4] *Capital*, vol. II, London, 1961, p. 158.

140

'older' machine is more efficient than a 'younger' one:

'Take, for example, a machine which lasts twelve years and costs £12,000; its average wear and tear, which has to be charged each year, amounts to £1,000. . . . In fact, however, reality differs from this calculation of averages. The machine may perhaps run more smoothly in the second year than in the first.'[5]

Thus Marx worked in terms of linear value depreciation but was aware that it was an oversimplification.

Since partially used fixed capital will be treated below as a joint product, it may be of interest to note that Marx was familiar with this procedure (though he did not, unfortunately, make use of it). It is stated quite explicitly in a passage by Torrens which Marx quoted at length[6] and Marx himself discussed it in *Capital*, vol. I, where he also quoted Malthus as writing that 'If we reckon the value of the fixed capital employed as a part of the advances, we must reckon the remaining value of such capital at the end of the year as a part of the annual return'. While Torrens and Malthus were perfectly correct on this particular point, Marx unfortunately did not adopt their approach, arguing (incorrectly) that it is adequate to subtract 'the remaining value' from both sides of the value accounts, leaving in only the net depreciation figure.[7]

A simple fixed capital using economy

Consider then a very simple capitalist economy, undergoing simple reproduction, in which the only products are corn and a machine. The new machine is made by labour, using only corn as an input; no pretence of realism will be made in this example![8] The production process for making a machine out of corn takes one year. New

---

[5] *Theories of Surplus Value*, Part II, London, 1969, p. 479.
[6] *Theories of Surplus Value*, Part III, London, 1972, pp. 71–2.
[7] *Capital*, vol. I, pp. 320–1.
[8] More realistic assumptions would not alter the general conclusions to be drawn but would merely complicate the analysis.

machines are then used, together with some corn input, to produce further corn over the course of a year. Again, one-year old machines are used, together with corn input, to produce corn over the course of a second year. After two years' use, the machine becomes useless.

The quantities of corn and labour-time, and the numbers of new and old machines, entering and leaving the three different processes of production are shown in Table I.

Table I

	Corn	New	Old	Labour	Corn	New	Old
	C_1	O	O	L_1 →	O	M	O
	C_2	M	O	L_2 →	Q_2	O	M
	C_3	O	M	L_3 →	Q_3	O	O
Total	C	M	M	L →	Q	M	M

Thus the first row shows that C_1 units of corn are used by L_1 units of labour-time to produce M *new* machines, while the second row shows that C_2 units of corn and M *new* machines are used by L_2 units of labour-time to produce Q_2 units of corn (gross) *plus*, of course, M one-year *old* machines. In the third row, L_3 units of labour-time are shown to use C_3 units of corn and M *old* machines to produce Q_3 units of corn (gross). The final (total) row, which refers to the economy as a whole, simply shows that, in aggregate, $C(= C_1 + C_2 + C_3)$ units of corn, M new machines, M old machines and $L(= L_1 + L_2 + L_3)$ units of labour time are used to produce $Q(= Q_1 + Q_2)$ units of corn, M new machines and M old machines.

It will be noted that, for both new and old machines, the number 'produced' is exactly equal to the number used up, namely M, so that simple reproduction is ensured as far as machines are concerned. The *net* output of the system is just $(Q - C)$ units of corn; obviously $Q > C$ for a meaningful economic system. If this net product is divided in the same way between wages and profits every year, then simple reproduction will result. It is also to be noted that the new and old machines may or may not be of equal efficiency in the production of corn, depending on the quantities C_2, L_2, Q_2, C_3, L_3 and Q_3 in Table I.

An example with rising efficiency
Suppose that Table I takes the particular numerical values shown in Table II.

Table II

	Corn	New	Old	Labour	Corn	New	Old
	1	0	0	5 →	0	5	0
	9	5	0	10 →	10	0	5
	15	0	5	25 →	25	0	0
Total	25	5	5	40 →	35	5	5

It will be seen from the second and third rows of Table II that, while gross corn output per unit of labour-time is the same in each case, corn input and machine input per unit of gross corn output are both *lower* in the third row, i.e., the old machine using process is more efficient than the new machine using process. This phenomenon, which as noted above was referred to by Marx, might be the result of the 'running-in' of the new machine.

Marx's value calculation
In Table II, the total labour-time expended is 40 units, while the *net* product is $(35-25) = 10$ units of corn. The value of each unit of

corn, l_c, is thus given by

$$10l_c = 40$$

or

$$l_c = 4. \tag{1}^9$$

Using (1), the application of Marx's 'value $= c+v+s$' formula to the first row of Table II shows that the value of each *new* machine, l_n, is given by

$$l_c + 5 = 5l_n$$

or

$$4 + 5 = 5l_n$$

or

$$l_n = 1.8. \tag{2}$$

Now, according to Marx's linear depreciation approach, since the machine lasts just two years the value of an old machine, l_o, should be

$$l_o = \tfrac{1}{2}l_n = 0.9,$$

and the fixed capital depreciation element of 'constant capital value' should be 0.9 per machine in both the new and the old machine using process. Marx's value accounts for the second and third rows of Table II would thus be:

(second row) $\qquad 9l_c + 5(0.9) + 10 = 10l_c$

or

$$l_c = 14.5 \tag{3}$$

and (third row) $\qquad 15l_c + 5(0.9) + 25 = 25l_c$

or

$$l_c = 2.95. \tag{4}$$

[9] l_c will be calculated in an alternative way below.

144

Now 'results' (3) and (4) are not merely different from (1) above; they are *mutually inconsistent*. Marx's assumption of linear value depreciation has led to a nonsensical result.

Correct value accounting

The joint production approach, starting from the physical data of Table II, leads easily to the derivation of consistent magnitudes for l_c, l_n and l_o. Applying the 'value $= c + v + s$' formula to each of the first three rows yields:

$$\text{(first row)} \qquad l_c + 5 = 5l_n \qquad\qquad (5)$$

$$\text{(second row)} \qquad 9l_c + 5l_n + 10 = 10l_c + 5l_o \qquad (6)$$

$$\text{(third row)} \qquad 15l_c + 5l_o + 25 = 25l_c \qquad (7)$$

Relations (5), (6) and (7) entail that:

$$l_c = 4,\ l_n = 1.8,\ l_o = 3. \qquad (8)^{10}$$

It will be noted that the solutions for l_c and l_n, in (8), are just those obtained before by a different method. More significant is the fact that l_o has now been determined as well. What may be surprising is that the correct value of $l_o(= 3)$ is not only different from the value implied by Marx's reasoning $(= 0.9)$ but is actually *greater* than l_n: the old machine has a *greater* value than the new one, so that the correct 'value depreciation' in the new machine using process $(= l_n - l_o = -1.2)$ is actually *negative*.

This example suffices to show that Marx's assumption of linear value depreciation is incorrect, in general, and that, with machines of rising efficiency, value depreciation *can* be negative.[11]

[10] The reader may check this solution by substitution; there is no alternative solution.

[11] It does not, of course, establish that value depreciation *has* to be negative with rising efficiency. In fact it is easy to show, from Table I, that $l_o \gtreqless l_n$ according as

$$L_2 \cdot L \gtreqless (Q_2 - C_2)(Q - C).$$

An example with falling efficiency

Suppose now that Table I takes the values shown in Table III. The old machine using process (row three) is now less efficient than the new machine using process (row two), in that the *net* corn product of 3 machines and 30 units of labour is 27 units in the former but 39 units in the latter.

Table III

Corn	New	Old	Labour		Corn	New	Old
3	0	0	3	→	0	3	0
49	3	0	30	→	88	0	3
3	0	3	30	→	30	0	0
Total 55	3	3	63	→118	3	3

The values l_c, l_n and l_o are determined, in Marx's accounting, by applying the 'c + v + s' formula to each row in turn to obtain:

(first row) $$3l_c + 3 = 3l_n \qquad (9)$$

(second row) $$49l_c + 3l_n + 30 = 88l_c + 3l_o \qquad (10)$$

(third row) $$3l_c + 3l_o + 30 = 30l_c. \qquad (11)$$

Relations (9), (10) and (11) yield the (unique) solutions:

$$l_c = 1, \; l_n = 2, \; l_o = -1. \qquad (12)$$

(Since the *net* product of the system, using 63 units of labour, is just $63(= 118 - 55)$ units of corn, the result $l_c = 1$ could have been read off directly from Table III.) In the present example, l_o is indeed less than l_n but is actually *negative*. Marx's additive value accounts, consistently applied, [12] impute a negative embodied labour content

---

[12] As in the first numerical example, with l_c determined from the *total* row for the economy as a whole, the first row of Table III suffices to determine $l_n = 2$. Marx's assumption that $l_o = \frac{1}{2}l_n = 1$, however, produces incoherent results when applied to the second and third rows of Table III.

to each old machine.[13] Such a negative value can be given a meaningful interpretation, as will be seen in the next chapter, but one is entitled to wonder whether it conveys what Marx had in mind by the value of an old machine. Thus in the old machine using process (row three of Table III), Marx's 'value of constant capital' comes out as $(3l_c + 3l_o) = 0$.

Profits and prices of production

Since the derivative value magnitudes are of no essential significance in the determination of the profit rate, it is not to be expected that the negative l_o value derived above will imply any difficulty in that determination. One simply proceeds directly from the physical data of Table III and a given, real corn wage rate. Let the latter be $(2/3)$ of a unit of corn per unit of labour-time. Then if wages are paid in advance, the rate of profit, r, and the production prices of new and old machines[14] relative to the price of corn, p_n and p_o respectively, are determined by:

$$(1+r)(3+2) = 3p_n \tag{13}$$

$$(1+r)(49+3p_n+20) = 88+3p_o \tag{14}$$

$$(1+r)(3+3p_o+20) = 30. \tag{15}$$

It will be noted that each labour quantity in Table III has been multiplied by the wage-rate of $(2/3)$ and that (14) incorporates the joint production treatment of the old machine. Relations (13), (14) and (15) may be solved to obtain:

$$r = 20\%, \ p_n = 2, \ p_o = (2/3). \tag{16}$$

[13] This example does not, of course, establish that l_o *must* be negative with falling efficiency. It follows from Table I that

$$l_o \gtreqless 0 \text{ according as } L_3 \cdot L \gtreqless (Q_3 - C_3)(Q \dot- C).$$

[14] p_o is always the correct 'book value' of an old machine; if there is a fully developed market in old machines, with no transaction or transport costs, then it will also be the price at which old machines are bought and sold.

The profit rate and production prices in (16) have been determined directly from the physical conditions of production and the real wage, no value magnitude – even one which does follow correctly from Table III – being of any relevance to that determination.

Choice of technique

The above determination of r implicitly assumes the (correct) answer to a question which has not so far been raised; will the old machine using process actually be used? This is an important question, for it would be technically possible for the capitalists simply to scrap the machine after only one year of use, reallocating the labour-time and corn shown in the third row of Table III to the production of new machines and to the production of corn, using new machines. Assuming constant returns to scale, the rate of profit, r, would then be given by:

$$(1+r)(3+2) = 3p_n \qquad (17)$$

$$(1+r)(49+3p_n+20) = 88, \qquad (18)$$

p_o now being *zero*, since the one-year old machine is scrapped. However, (17) and (18) imply that

$$r = 17.6\%, p_n = 1.96,$$

so that a *lower* rate of profit would result from not using the old machine using process. Thus we were in fact justified in assuming above that all three processes are used.

This is far from meaning, however, that the question raised here is unimportant. It makes the general point that fixed capital always introduces a particular kind of 'choice of technique' problem for capitalists, namely, for how many years should a machine be used. It will not have been forgotten, from chapter 4, that when there is a choice of technique, the determination of the profit rate is *logically prior* to the determination of value magnitudes. Thus *the presence of fixed capital means that the determination of the profit rate is logically prior to that of values*, whether or not there is any other kind of choice over the methods of production.

It may be noted, in fact, that if the wage rate, rather than being (2/3), were greater than 0.8 (approximately), then a higher rate of profit would indeed be yielded by scrapping the machine after one year's use. If the fact that the old machine was not used were then taken to entail that $l_o = 0$, the first rows of Table III would imply that:

$$3l_c + 3 = 3l_n$$

and

$$49l_c + 3l_n + 30 = 88l_c$$

which yield the values

$$l_c = (11/12), l_n = (23/12).$$

If l_o were *not* taken to be zero, on the other hand, then l_c, l_n and l_o would be indeterminate. Either way, then, the values of the commodities are not determined to be the same when the wage exceeds 0.8 as when it equals (2/3). The embodied labour-time values are not only derivative of the physical conditions of production and the real wage but they *depend on* the level of the given wage.[15] In the presence of fixed capital, value magnitudes are completely devoid of any significance for the determination of the rate of profit. The physical quantities approach, however, can analyse fixed capital *and* the general kind of choice of technique, with ease.

Conclusion

If value magnitudes are to be calculated in Marx's additive way in fixed capital using systems, then they must be calculated, from the physical data, using the joint products approach. Marx's linear

---

[15] It was not necessary to consider the choice of technique problem in our first example because, the old machine being *more* efficient than the new one and being so only by virtue of the latter's being used, it could not possibly be more profitable to drop the use of *either* machine using process.

value depreciation assumption is not acceptable, for it can lead to incoherent results. When properly calculated, additive values can prove to be negative for old machines or, if positive, greater than the values of the corresponding new machines.

More fundamental, however, is the point that there is no useful purpose to be served by calculating Marx's additive value magnitudes at all. They are mere derivates of the physical data and the latter suffice to determine the rate of profit and all prices of production. Indeed, in the presence of fixed capital, the choice of the optimal life of a machine is determined only in the course of maximizing the rate of profit, so that the value magnitudes, which depend on the effective life of the machine, are determined only *after* the profit rate is determined. The physical conditions of production and the real wage are the proximate determinants of the profit rate. The task is to show what determines those physical production conditions and real wages, not to engage in pointless value calculations.

11

Positive Profits with Negative Surplus Value

It was seen in the previous chapter that when fixed capital is correctly analysed as a particular case of joint production, Marx's additive value accounts can impute to an old machine a positive, a zero or even a negative value. It will be shown in the present chapter that 'pure' joint production can lead to similar results, even in the absence of fixed capital. The fact that Marx's additive value accounts, with 'value = c + v + s', can impute positive, zero or negative values to commodities in the joint production context, will be emphasized here by constructing an example in which the bundle of commodities appropriated by the capitalists actually has a negative value in aggregate. That is, surplus value, defined as total living labour *minus* the total labour embodied in the workers' real wages – where each commodity value is defined in Marx's additive way – will be found to be negative, even though the rate of profit and prices of production will be found to be positive.

The implication of this result should be clear enough: commodity values and surplus value, as Marx defined them, are not merely irrelevant to the determination of the profit rate (and prices of production) but actually lead to results which deprive such value magnitudes of any significance which Marx might have sought to attribute to them. Marx's concept of additively defined values should be abandoned.[1]

[1] While a simple numerical example will suffice for the purposes of this chapter, some more general relevant remarks will be found in chapter 12. I

The assumptions

Consider a capitalist economy undergoing steady growth, without technical progress, in which workers save nothing, while capitalists have a savings ratio of unity. There are two additive, divisible, constant returns to scale processes of production, which have the same production period; this period will be taken as the time unit for the analysis. There are two commodities, both of which serve as inputs to production and are fully used up in one period. It is assumed, that is, that capital is circulating capital, fixed capital being absent. Both processes, however, are joint-production processes, producing positive quantities of each commodity. Exchange of commodities takes place, at the end of each period, on fully competitive markets. Wages are paid at the end of the period; they do not depend on the supply of homogeneous labour, which is always at least equal to the demand. Table I shows the commodity inputs to and outputs obtained from each process when it is operated by one unit of labour under the prevailing technical and social conditions; inputs being shown to the left of the arrows and outputs to the right.

Table I

	Commodity 1	Commodity 2	Labour		Commodity 1	Commodity 2
Process 1	5	0	1	→	6	1
Process 2	0	10	1	→	3	12

may also be noted that the example given here can be seen as a simple case of the von Neumann analysis discussed in chapter 13. Reference will be made in this chapter to M. Morishima, *Marx's Economics. A Dual Theory of Value and Growth*, Cambridge, 1973, to M. Morishima, 'Marx in the Light of Modern Economic Theory', *Econometrica*, 1974 and to P. Sraffa, *Production of Commodities by Means of Commodities*, Cambridge, 1960. It must also be stated that the chapter has been influenced by G. Gilibert, 'Produzione Congiunta e Valori-Lavoro Negativi' (unpublished) and by B. Schefold, *Mr. Sraffa on Joint Production*, privately published in Basel, 1971.

The price system

We assume that the real wage bundle contains, for every 6 units of labour, 3 units of the first commodity and 5 of the second. This given real wage, together with the production conditions, will determine the profit rate and commodity prices. Given our assumptions about savings behaviour, the growth rate will also be determined, being equal to the profit rate.

Let the labour commanded by a unit of the first (second) commodity be $p_1(p_2)$ and the uniform profit rate be r. Then, from Table I, the following relations must hold:

$$(1+r)5p_1 + 1 = 6p_1 + p_2 \tag{1}$$

$$(1+r)10p_2 + 1 = 3p_1 + 12p_2. \tag{2}$$

Furthermore, the real wage bundle which is purchased by 6 units of labour must command 6 units of labour, so that:

$$3p_1 + 5p_2 = 6. \tag{3}$$

As the reader may check by substitution, the solutions to (1), (2) and (3) are:[2]

$$r = 20\%, \ p_1 = \tfrac{1}{3}, \ p_2 = 1.$$

Note that the profit rate and the prices are all positive.

The quantity system

Suppose that, in a certain period, 6 units of labour are employed, 5 operating the first process and 1 operating the second. The resulting input and output flows for this period will be as shown in Table II, where the third row shows the economy-wide situation resulting from the simultaneous operation of the two processes. This situation is consistent with steady growth, at a rate equal to the profit rate. To see this, consider Tables II and III together. Total material input is

[2] As the reader may also check by substitution, there is an alternative solution, namely $r = 1.6\%$, $p_1 = -12/19$, $p_2 = 30/19$. The negative price p_1 makes this solution economically insignificant.

(25 + 10) and net investment is (5 + 2); clearly (5 + 2) = 20%
(25 + 10). Thus net investment is just that required for steady growth
at a rate equal to the profit rate.

Table II

	Com-modity 1	Com-modity 2	Labour	Com-modity 1	Com-modity 2
Process 1	25	0	5 →	30	5
Process 2	0	10	1 →	3	12
Total	25	10	6 →	33	17

From the price and quantity systems, it will be seen that all
inputs and outputs, prices, wages and growth and profit rates are
positive. Hence nothing abnormal would be observed in our
economy.

Table III

	Commodity 1		Commodity 2
Net product	8	+	7
Wage bundle	3	+	5
Net investment	5	+	2

The value system

We now derive the value of each commodity, i.e. the quantity of
labour required, directly and indirectly, to produce each unit of net
output of that commodity. With joint production one cannot follow

the method of reduction to dated labour, for one cannot directly allocate the labour input to a process between the two outputs. Instead, one must have recourse to a simultaneous determination of values. Let the value of the first (second) commodity be $l_1(l_2)$. Then we see from Table I that

$$5l_1 + 1 = 6l_1 + l_2 \tag{4}$$

$$10l_2 + 1 = 3l_1 + 12l_2. \tag{5}$$

As the reader may check by substitution, the solution to (4) and (5) is:[3]

$$l_1 = -1, l_2 = 2.$$

We can now calculate V, the 'value of labour power', that is the labour embodied in the wage bundle, and the 'surplus value' S, which is the labour embodied in the bundle of commodities (net of replacement) appropriated by the capitalists. If the calculations are correct we must, of course, find that $(V + S) = 6 =$ total labour employed. Now the bundle of commodities appropriated by the workers is $(3 + 5)$, while that appropriated by the capitalists is $(5 + 2)$. Hence

$$V = 3 \times (-1) + 5 \times 2 = 7$$

$$S = 5 \times (-1) + 2 \times 2 = -1$$

$$V + S = 6.$$

Thus surplus value is negative $(S = -1)$, while the rate of profit is positive $(r = 20\%)$. In a footnote a numerical example is given in which surplus value is positive, while the growth and profit rates are negative.[4] We conclude that, with joint production, the existence of positive surplus value is neither a necessary nor a sufficient condition

[3] Note that $(l_2/l_1) = -2$ while $(p_2/p_1) = 3$. Thus relative price can diverge from relative value not only in magnitude but also in sign.

[4] To provide a counter-example to the assertion that positive surplus value is a sufficient condition for positive profit, we must construct a case in which surplus value is positive but profits are negative. Since capitalists could, in fact, choose to obtain a zero profit rather than a negative one, simply by ceasing to be capitalists, it will be clear that the example is of a purely formal nature.

for the existence of positive profits, *when Marx's additive definition of value is adopted.*[5]

It has not been argued, it should be noted carefully, that with joint production surplus value and profit must be of opposite sign; we have merely shown that they can be. Returning to the section 'The price system', it will be clear that any real wage bundle $(w_1 + w_2)$ which satisfies the relation

$$\left(\frac{1}{3}\right)w_1 + w_2 = 6 \tag{6}$$

Consider then an economy with the same available processes and the same savings behaviour as assumed in the text. Let the real wage bundle be $(20.5 + 12)$ for every 6 units of labour. Equations (1) and (2) of the text will still apply but (3) must be replaced by

$$20.5p_1 + 12p_2 = 6. \tag{3'}$$

As the reader can check by substitution, the solution to (1), (2) and (3') is

$$r = -50\%, p_1 = 12/43, p_2 = 1/43.$$

(There is also an economically irrelevant solution, namely that given in footnote 2 above.) It can also be seen that the quantity system given in Table II of the text is compatible with steady growth at the rate of -50%, for the net output of $(8 + 7)$ minus the wage bundle of $(20.5 + 12)$ leaves $[(-12.5) + (-5)]$ for net investment and the latter is clearly $-50\%(25 + 10)$ or -50% of the material inputs. We can now calculate V and S:

$$V = 20.5 \times (-1) + 12 \times 2 = 3.5$$

$$S = (-12.5) \times (-1) + (-5) \times 2 = 2.5$$

$$V + S = 6.$$

Thus we have positive surplus value (S = 2.5) but negative profits (r = -50%) with positive prices. Hence positive surplus value is not a sufficient condition for positive profits.

[5] In his inaugural lecture (1974) Morishima has shown that 'Positive exploitation is necessary and sufficient . . . to guarantee capitalists positive profits.' This result may appear to be in stark contrast with ours but there is, in fact, *no* inconsistency between the two results, since Morishima adopts definitions of surplus and exploitation quite different from those used above. For an explanation – and advocacy – of Morishima's approach, see chapter 13 below.

will be consistent with the solution $r = +20\%$, $p_1 = \frac{1}{3}$, $p_2 = 1$. The corresponding values of S and V will be given by

$$V = -w_1 + 2w_2 \tag{7}$$

$$S = 6 - V = 6 + w_1 - 2w_2. \tag{8}$$

From (6), (7), (8) we see that

$$V = 5w_2 - 18$$

and

$$S = 24 - 5w_2,$$

where $0 \leqq w_2 \leqq 6$. The rate of surplus value, or rate of exploitation, e is defined by $e \equiv S/V$ so that

$$e = (24 - 5w_2)/(5w_2 - 18)$$

for $0 \leqq w_2 \leqq 6$. It is easy to show that as w_2 is notionally varied between 0 and 6, e takes on every value, from minus to plus infinity, except that it never falls in the open interval $(-4/3, -1/2)$. Hence almost every value of the rate of exploitation, positive or negative, is consistent with $r = +20\%$.

While we are considering the value system, it may be of interest to convert Table II to a set of 'value accounts' in which inputs and outputs are 'valued' in terms of embodied labour. As is usual in Marxist analysis, let C denote labour embodied in the produced means of production; we use W to denote the value of gross output. Then if we apply the results obtained above $[l_1 = -1, l_2 = 2, V = 7, S = (-1)]$, we obtain Table IV from Table II. In addition to surplus value being negative for each process and in total, both C, the 'value of constant capital', and W are negative for process one, while C is negative for the economy as a whole; in total, the produced means of production embody a negative amount of labour. Further, the 'value composition of capital', i.e. C/V, is negative for process one and for the economy as a whole.

Table IV

	C	V	S	W
Process 1	$-25 + 35/6 + (-5/6)$			$= (-20)$
Process 2	$20 + 7/6 + (-1/6)$			$= 21$
Total	$-5 + 7 + (-1)$			$= 1$

Discussion

Since the above numerical results may appear somewhat strange, it may be helpful to provide an intuitive interpretation of negative value and negative surplus value. One reason for finding 'negative value' rather odd, is that one is used to thinking of the Marxian value of a commodity as the labour required to produce a net output consisting of that commodity alone. Reflection will show, however, that with joint production it is, in general, not possible to produce only one commodity, this being so even if all values are positive. Consider Fig. I, where A, B are the net output points for two different processes. The downward slope of AB shows that both commodities have positive value. By appropriately allocating labour between the processes, net outputs lying on AB can be produced but points C and D, with only one commodity being produced, cannot be reached. A purely formal solution exists, it is true; C can be reached by allocating a positive amount of labour to process OA and a negative amount of labour to process OB, the difference between these two amounts of labour being the value of OC units of commodity 2. (A parallel argument holds for commodity 1.) Even though each commodity has a positive value, it is not sensible to think of these values as quantities of labour required to produce only the given commodity, since such production involves (meaningless) negative employment in one process. (If a commodity has a negative value, as in our example, this simply means that the hypothetical negative employment in one process outweighs the positive employment, in the other process.) Once it is seen that, with joint production, one should not conceive of the value of a commodity as the labour required to produce one unit of that commodity alone, the 'oddness' of a negative value disappears.

A more appropriate way to conceive of value is as the change in employment resulting from a change in net output from (y_1, y_2) to $(y_1 + 1, y_2)$ or $(y_1, y_2 + 1)$, where each net output *can* be produced by some meaningful, positive allocation of labour between the

Figure I

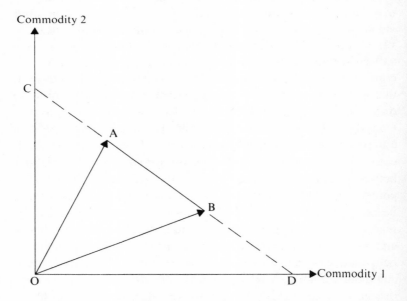

processes.[6] We have seen above that our economy, growing at 20% and paying a wage of $(3 + 5)$ to 6 units of labour, produces a net output – that is, wages plus net investment – of $(8 + 7)$. Now consider

[6] Cf. Sraffa, *op. cit.*, p. 60, second paragraph, and Morishima, *op. cit.*, (1973), p. 18: '. . . values are not more than the employment multipliers discussed by Kahn and later by Keynes. . . .'

another economy, with the same methods of production and also growing at 20%, and suppose that the real wage paid to 5 units of labour is $(6+3)$. It is easy to show that net output in this economy will be $(9+7)$. Thus, by comparison with the first economy, the second has the same net output of commodity 2, yet produces one more unit of commodity 1, even though employment is one unit smaller. This is the meaning of the result that commodity 1 has a value of -1. Again, consider a third economy, with the same methods of production and growing at 20%, which pays a real wage of $(3+6)$ to 7 units of labour; the net output will be $(9+8)$. By comparison with the second economy, the third economy produces the same net output of commodity 1 but one more unit of commodity 2 and employs two more units of labour. This is the meaning of the result that commodity 2 has a value of $+2$. Thus, if additive values are conceived of in a way which has meaning in the context of joint production, there is nothing at all strange about a negative value. It follows that there is nothing strange about negative surplus value.[7]

In Fig. II point $I_1(I_2)$ shows the input pattern that would obtain if 6 units of labour were allocated to process 1 (2), while point $N_1(N_2)$ shows the corresponding net output pattern. Naturally, all the points on the straight line $N_1 N_2$ are possible net output patterns with total employment equal to 6. The fact that $N_1 N_2$ has a positive slope shows immediately that commodities one and two have values of opposite sign. The points I and N show the input and net output patterns displayed in Table II.

Point W in Fig. II shows the wage bundle $(3+5)$. Since W lies above the extension of $N_1 N_2$, it follows that the real wage bundle embodies more than 6 units of labour and hence that additive surplus value is negative.[8]

[7] Provided, that is, that Marx's *additive* value accounts are retained. See chapter 13 below for Morishima's alternative approach in which negative value magnitudes are impossible, by definition.
[8] Note that the wage bundle $(3+5)$, at W, could not be produced *exactly* by *any* amount of labour, since it lies outside the cone defined by N_1, N_2 and the origin.

Figure II

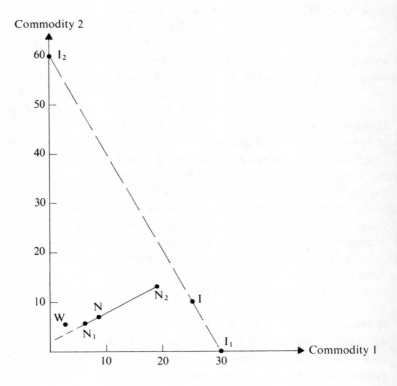

Commodity 2

Commodity 1

An implicit assumption

It was taken for granted in the argument above that both processes
were operated at a positive level. Yet since the first process produces
a net output of only $(1+1)$ when operated with one unit of labour,
while the second process, with the same employment, produces a
net output of $(3+2)$, it might be questioned whether the first process
will be used.

Returning to Table I, if process 1 is operated by 6 units of labour
which are paid a real wage of $(3+5)$, the condition that super-
normal profits, over and above the profits at rate r, should be

negative or zero can be written as

$$30p_1(1+r) + 3p_1 + 5p_2 \geqq 36p_1 + 6p_2$$

or

$$30p_1 r \geqq 3p_1 + p_2. \tag{9}$$

In the same way, for process 2,

$$60p_2(1+r) + 3p_1 + 5p_2 \geqq 18p_1 + 72p_2$$

or

$$60p_2 r \geqq 15p_1 + 7p_2. \tag{10}$$

Now p_1 and p_2 cannot both be zero; we therefore see from (9) that p_1 cannot be zero and from (10) that p_2 cannot be zero. Hence, in a competitive equilibrium, both p_1 and p_2 must be positive and therefore excess demand for each commodity must be exactly zero. Each process, however, produces a positive supply of both commodities, even after the wage bundle has been subtracted, but uses only one commodity as an input. Thus, given our assumptions about savings, it is impossible for either process alone to generate a zero excess demand for each commodity. Hence if a competitive equilibrium exists, it must involve the operation of both processes. We have, of course, already given an example of such an equilibrium above.[9]

Conclusion

In the presence of joint production, Marx's additive value accounts can impute positive or negative values to individual commodities. It follows that the aggregate value of the commodities appropriated by the capitalists, i.e. total surplus value, can be negative, even when

[9] It may be noted that positive growth is not essential for the conclusion that negative value is consistent with positive profits and prices. Suppose, for example, that capitalists save nothing and consume the commodities in the fixed proportions of five units of commodity 1 for every two units of commodity 2. A competitive equilibrium will exist with exactly the same prices, quantities and additive values as given in the text.

the rate of profit and all prices of production are positive. Since it has already been seen in chapter 4 that Marx's additive value magnitudes are completely irrelevant to the determination of the profit rate (and prices of production), there appears to be no good reason for not abandoning all reference to such magnitudes, it being clearly understood that such an abandonment in no way leads to the rejection of a materialist account of capitalist economies and their working. The physical data concerning production conditions and real wages can explain anything explicable in terms of value magnitudes, which are merely their derivates, and can indeed explain far more. Marxists should therefore concentrate on developing the materialist account of why production conditions and real wages are what they are, leaving the discussion of 'value magnitudes' to those concerned only with the development of a new Gnosticism.

12

An Analysis of Fixed Capital and Joint Production

The simple numerical examples of chapters 10 and 11 have shown that the presence of fixed capital or pure joint products can give rise to certain problems not encountered in the analysis of single-product, circulating capital systems. This chapter will present a method of treating the analysis of fixed capital and pure joint products in a general way, which both subsumes all our previous analyses as special cases and leads into the arguments considered in the next chapter. The analysis of the choice between alternative production methods will indeed be left over for discussion in the following chapter, attention being focussed here on the analysis of a given set of n productive processes in which n commodities are produced, whether singly or jointly.[1]

---

[1] It will be recalled that, in the present context, the choice of production method includes the choice of how many years fixed capital should be used: *cf*. chapter 10. With joint production processes it is, of course, technically possible for the number of products to exceed the number of processes used. It can be shown, however, that the profit maximizing choice of production methods will, in general, lead to the use of a number of methods *exactly equal* to the number of products *having a positive price*. Thus if only such products are regarded as *commodities* (waste smoke from a furnace is a technical product but is not a commodity) then it may be said that, in general, the number of production methods will be equal to the number of commodities. *Cf*., Ian Steedman, 'Positive Profits with Negative Surplus Value: A Reply to Wolfstetter', *Economic Journal*, 1976.

The output matrix

As in our earlier analyses, let the jth column of the (n × n) matrix A
represent the commodity inputs used in production process j and
let the row vector a represent the quantities of labour-time used in
the various production processes, all of which take one 'year'. In
the single-product, circulating capital economy it is, of course
possible simply to identify the jth production process with the jth
industry and to represent the output of the jth industry as one unit
of commodity j. In those simple economies, then, the 'output matrix'
is just an (n × n) matrix with unit elements along the main diagonal
and zeros everywhere else, i.e., an identity matrix. When there is
fixed capital, however, each 'industry' will contain many different
productive processes. For processes have to be distinguished by the
age of the fixed capital goods being used. At the same time, the
'outputs' from a fixed capital using process will, in general, be at
least two in number (the product in the everyday sense and the
one-year older machine(s)) so that the matrix of outputs is obviously
no longer a diagonal matrix. When there are pure joint products it
is, again, apparent that the output matrix cannot be diagonal and,
indeed, the very concept of 'an industry' may become less sharply
defined, even though the individual productive processes are well
defined.

The implication of the above is, of course, that in analysing a
fixed capital using and/or pure joint product producing system, one
must define not just the input matrix, A, and the labour input vector
a, but also the (n × n) matrix of outputs, B say. The jth column of B
represents the quantities of commodities produced by production
method j, where that list of commodities is taken to include all
partially used items of fixed capital. (Thus machines, etc., of
different ages are treated as *distinct* commodities and are represented
as such in the columns of both A and B.)

Direct and indirect production requirements

By definition, A and a show the direct material and labour inputs to the productive processes whose outputs are represented by B. It may now be asked what quantities of commodities and of labour-time are required, directly *and indirectly*, for the production of one unit of *net* product of each commodity.

Let the row vector l represent the quantities of labour-time required, whether directly or indirectly, in the production of one unit of each commodity, i.e., the vector of values. Marx's additive value accounts (value of gross product = value of inputs), when applied to each productive process in turn, imply that

$$lB = lA + a$$

or

$$l = a(B - A)^{-1}. \tag{1}$$

Relation (1) determines the values, l, in terms of the physical conditions of production, represented by A, a and B.

In the case of a single-product, circulating capital system, B can be made equal to the identity matrix, so that (1) may be written as

$$l = a(I - A)^{-1}. \tag{2}$$

If A, a in (2) represent a meaningful economic system, capable of generating positive profits, then the l vector determined by (2) is necessarily strictly positive. The analogous result *does not hold*, however, for the far more general (and economically important) case represented by (1). The economic meaningfulness of the system A, a, B does not guarantee that the vector l determined by (1) is strictly positive; it may or may not be. (It will be recalled that in the first example of chapter 10 and in Figure I of chapter 11 both commodities had positive values, while in the second example of chapter 10 and in the numerical example of chapter 11 one commodity had a negative value.) Thus, in the presence of fixed capital and/or pure joint products, Marx's additive value accounts may or may not impute negative values to certain commodities.[2]

---

[2] If the *only* joint products are old machines then, under certain assumptions, old machines are the only commodities to which negative values may be imputed.

It is also to be noted that, in general, the right-hand side of relation (1) cannot be expanded as a power series to present the value vector, l, as the sum of an infinite series of 'dated' labour input vectors. While (2) may be expanded as

$$l = a + a\mathbf{A} + a\mathbf{A}^2 + \ldots$$

if a, $\mathbf{A}$ are economically meaningful,[3] the expansion of (1) as

$$l = a\mathbf{B}^{-1}[\mathbf{I} + (\mathbf{A}\mathbf{B}^{-1}) + (\mathbf{A}\mathbf{B}^{-1})^2 + \ldots]$$

is not necessarily legitimate, even for economically meaningful a, $\mathbf{A}$, $\mathbf{B}$; $(\mathbf{A}\mathbf{B}^{-1})$ need not be a non-negative matrix, the terms $(\mathbf{A}\mathbf{B}^{-1})^t$ need not eventually tend to the null matrix as t tends to infinity and 'the dated labour input vector' $[a\mathbf{B}^{-1}(\mathbf{A}\mathbf{B}^{-1})^t]$ can have negative elements, for which no economic meaning is apparent. Hence the dated labour analysis must be abandoned as soon as one leaves the over simple world of single-product, circulating capital systems.[4] This does not, of course, constitute any problem for the Sraffa-based analysis since, as was pointed out in chapter 5, dated labour analysis is not at all central to it.

Consider now the question of what physical capital stocks are used, directly or indirectly, in the production of one unit (net) of each commodity.[5] Let the column vector of physical capital stocks be denoted by h and the column vector of *net* output be denoted by y. If e is the (n × 1) column vector each of whose elements is unity then h, which is the sum of the columns of $\mathbf{A}$, is given by

$$h = \mathbf{A}e, \tag{3}$$

while y, which is gross output *minus* h, is given by

$$y = \mathbf{B}e - h$$

[3] *Cf.*, chapter 5 above.

[4] While dated labour analysis is often applied directly to the price vector rather than to the value vector, the above arguments carry over immediately to that context.

[5] Physical capital stocks here do *not* include real wages.

or

$$y = (B-A)e. \qquad (4)$$

Provided that $(B-A)$ is non-singular,[6] (3) and (4) entail that

$$h = A(B-A)^{-1}y. \qquad (5)$$

Defining $H \equiv A(B-A)^{-1}$, (5) can be written as

$$h = Hy. \qquad (6)[7]$$

Thus if h_j is the jth column of H and y_j the jth element of y,

$$h = \Sigma_1^n y_j h_j,$$

so that (6) represents the actual capital stock vector, h, as the sum of n individual capital stock vectors of the form $y_j h_j$. In other words, h_j, the jth column of H, represents the vector of capital goods used, directly or indirectly, in the production of one unit (net) of commodity j. Thus the matrix $H \equiv A(B-A)^{-1}$ is the matrix of direct and indirect commodity capital inputs; it is the material input counterpart to the vector of direct and indirect labour requirements, l.

Just as l can have some negative elements when B cannot be made a diagonal matrix, so H can then have some negative elements. If, say, h_j has one or more such elements, this does *not*, of course, mean that some negative capital stocks would be required if the net output contained only commodity j; it means rather that net output *cannot* contain only commodity j. To illustrate the point involved, consider the numerical example of chapter 11, for which the H matrix is given

[6] $(B-A)$ can be singular in a system which is perfectly meaningful at a *positive* rate of profit. The equations $lB = lA + a$ are then either inconsistent or not such as to determine l uniquely. While the singularity of $(B-A)$ would necessarily prevent the particular form of presentation adopted here it would not, it should be noted, affect the determination of the profit rate in terms of the physical data.

[7] H is the symbol used by L. L. Pasinetti, who first drew attention to the significance of the matrix $A(B-A)^{-1}$ in his paper, 'The Notion of Vertical Integration in Economic Analysis', *Metroeconomica*, 1973.

by

$$H = \begin{bmatrix} -10 & 15 \\ 10 & -10 \end{bmatrix},$$

so that each column involves a negative entry. Assuming constant returns to scale, if the *net* outputs of commodities 1 and 2 are y_1 and y_2, then

$$h = \begin{bmatrix} -10 & 15 \\ 10 & -10 \end{bmatrix}\begin{pmatrix} y_1 \\ y_2 \end{pmatrix} = \begin{pmatrix} -10y_1 + 15y_2 \\ 10y_1 - 10y_2 \end{pmatrix}.$$

Thus both elements of h are non-negative if and only if $10y_2 \leqq 10y_1 \leqq 15y_2$ or $2y_2 \leqq 2y_1 \leqq 3y_2$. Thus (y_1/y_2) must lie between 1 and (3/2), which are precisely the ratios in which the two individual processes produce the net outputs. Hence for any non-zero net output (y_1, y_2) that can actually be produced, h will be semi-positive or positive. Similar reasoning will establish the same point in the more general context.

Before turning to the analysis of the profit rate (and prices of production), we may consider briefly how the above concepts would need to be modified if wages were advanced, the physical wage bundle being w. As in chapter 4, define the matrix

$$A^+ \equiv (A + w \cdot a),$$

where total employment, equal to $a \cdot e$, is here set equal to one by choice of units. The capital vector, which now includes the real wage bundle, will be given by

$$h^+ = A^+ \cdot e = (A \cdot e + w). \tag{7}$$

Net output, net that is of *both* used up means of production *and* real wages, will be given by

$$y^- = Be - h^+$$

or

$$y^- = (B - A^+) \cdot e. \tag{8}$$

Hence, provided only that $(B - A^+)$ is non-singular, (7) and (8) entail that

$$h^+ = A^+(B - A^+)^{-1}y^-$$ (9)

or

$$h^+ = H^+ \cdot y^-, \text{ say.}$$ (10)

The jth column of H^+ shows the capital stocks required, *inclusive* of real wages, for the direct and indirect production of each unit of j appropriated (net) by the capitalists.[8]

The rate of profit

Let the rate of profit per production period (per 'year') be r and let the row vector of prices of production, expressed in terms of labour commanded,[9] be p. Then if wages are paid *ex post*, we must have

$$pB = a + (1 + r)pA.$$ (11)

Hence

$$p = a[B - (1 + r)A]^{-1}.$$ (12)

Now the real wage bundle, w, 'commands' – exchanges with – the total labour-time employed,[10] $L = a \cdot e = 1$, so that $p \cdot w = L$ or, from (12),

$$a[B - (1 + r)A]^{-1}w = L.$$ (13)

Relation (13) determines the rate of profit, r, in terms of the physical conditions of production – expressed by a, B, A and L – and the real wage bundle, w. Relation (12) then determines the labour commanded price of production of each commodity, in terms of the same data. The physically based theory of the rate of profit provides a

---

[8] It may be noted that $H^+ \equiv (H + w \cdot l)(I - w \cdot l)^{-1}$.

[9] The use of labour commanded prices is convenient but in no way essential to the analysis.

[10] It is assumed here, as throughout, that workers do no saving.

170

proximate determination of that rate, no matter how many items of fixed capital there may be, nor how many pure joint products, no reference to any value magnitude being necessary.[11]

If wages are paid in advance, then relations (11), (12) and (13) will all continue to hold good, provided only that in each case a is multiplied by $(1+r)$. The profit rate (and prices of production) will still be determined by the conditions of production and the real wage.

Further on the rate of profit

While it has just been seen that no reference to value magnitudes is *necessary* in the proximate determination of the profit rate and prices of production – and naturally such derivative magnitudes can be no more significant in any ulterior determination – it may nevertheless be of interest to show how they *can be* referred to.

Relation (11) may be rewritten as

$$p(B-A) = a+rpA$$

or

$$p = a(B-A)^{-1}+rpA(B-A)^{-1}$$

or

$$p = l+rpH, \tag{14}$$

using (1) and the definition of H. As was pointed out by Pasinetti,[12] relation (14) shows that the labour commanded by any commodity $j(p_j)$ is equal to the labour embodied in that commodity (l_j) *plus* the profits on the labour commanded by the capital stocks required, directly or indirectly, in its production $(rp \cdot h_j)$. Solving (14), one

[11] The non-diagonal nature of B does, however, cause one complication which could not arise in the single-product, circulating capital case, namely that (12) and (13) need not necessarily yield a *unique* positive (r, p) solution. It will be seen in the following chapter how a unique solution for r can be ensured.

[12] *Op. cit.*, pp. 7–8.

obtains

$$p = l(I - rH)^{-1}. \tag{15}$$

Together with the relation $p \cdot w = L$, (15) yields

$$l(I - rH)^{-1}w = L \tag{16}$$

which is simply a rewritten version of (13), just as (15) is merely a rewriting of (12). Equation (16) determines r in terms of the conditions of production, now expressed by l, H and L, and real wages, w. Relation (15) then determines prices of production in terms of the same data.[13]

While (15) and (16) may be of interest, it must not be forgotten either that they are merely versions of (12) and (13), which make no reference to value magnitudes, or that (12) and (13) are more fundamental, both in the sense that a, A and B are needed for the derivation of l and H and in the sense that if $(B - A)$ should be singular, (15) and (16) fail to hold, while (12) and (13) are unaffected.

If wages are paid in advance then

$$pB = (1 + r)(pA + a)$$

or

$$pB = (1 + r)p(A + w \cdot a), \tag{17}$$

since $p \cdot w = 1$. Using the notation $A^+ \equiv (A + w \cdot a)$, (17) may be written as

$$pB = (1 + r)pA^+$$

or

$$p(B - A^+) = rpA^+$$

---

[13] If l and H are not semi-positive then non-unique solutions may arise, as mentioned in note 11 above. If l is not semi-positive then the set of methods of production considered will never actually be chosen at 'too low' a profit rate, for a 'low' rate of profit would, from (15), imply meaningless negative prices for one or more commodities. It will be seen from (15) that p will be proportional to l only if l is a characteristic vector of H.

or

$$p = \text{r}p\text{A}^+(\text{B}-\text{A}^+)^{-1}$$

or

$$p = \text{r}p \cdot \text{H}^+, \tag{18}$$

from (9) and (10). If H^+ is semi-positive, then (18) determines the rate of profit r as

$$\text{r}^{-1} = \lambda^{\text{PF}}(\text{H}^+). \tag{19}$$

If H^+ is not semi-positive, it can only be said that r^{-1} is a characteristic root of H^+, associated with a positive characteristic vector (to which p will naturally be proportional), so that r may not be uniquely determined by (18). In either case it is seen that r depends on the full detail of the direct and indirect capital stocks, including real wages, and not merely on direct and indirect labour requirements, let alone on simple value aggregates, such as S, C and V.

Exploitation

If wages are paid *ex post* then, since $p \cdot w = 1$, (14) may be written as

$$p = p(w \cdot l + \text{rH}). \tag{20}$$

If l and H are both semi-positive, it then follows from (20) that

$$\lambda^{\text{PF}}(w \cdot l + \text{rH}) = 1, \tag{21}$$

and that the condition for (21) to determine a positive value of r is that

$$\lambda^{\text{PF}}(w \cdot l) < 1.$$

But $\lambda^{\text{PF}}(w \cdot l) = l \cdot w = (1+\text{e})^{-1}$, where e is the rate of exploitation, so that $\text{e} > 0$ is the condition for $\text{r} > 0$ in (21). Thus if *l* and H are both semi-positive then, despite the presence of fixed capital and/or pure joint products, the profit rate will be positive if and only if the rate of exploitation is positive.[14]

If, on the other hand, l and/or H should contain one or more negative elements, the preceding argument becomes invalid. The simple numerical example in chapter 11 has already demonstrated that r *can* then be positive, with positive prices, even when the rate of exploitation, defined in terms of additive values, is negative.

If wages are paid in advance then (20) and (21) will still hold, provided that $w \cdot l$ is multiplied by $(1 + r)$; the rest of the above argument will be unaffected.

Marx's formula for the rate of profit

The foregoing sections have already established that fixed capital and/or pure joint products have no effect on the major thesis of this work; that the rate of profit (and prices of production) can be proximately determined in terms of the physically specified conditions of production and the real wage, no reference to any derivative value magnitudes being of the slightest significance to that determination. In this and the following sections use will be made of results obtained above to re-enforce and extend certain points, made in earlier chapters, concerning Marx's formula for the rate of profit, the labour process, heterogeneous labour and the treatment of circulation and turnover times.

Consider first Marx's formula for the rate of profit, which is $(S/C + V)$ if wages are advanced and (S/C) if they are paid *ex post*.[15] It was seen above, (14), that in the latter case

$$p = l + rp\mathrm{H};\qquad(22)$$

in the former case

$$p = (1 + r)l + rp\mathrm{H}.\qquad(23)$$

---

[14] As was pointed out in chapter 4, the positivity of e does not thereby become an *explanation* of the positivity of r; rather each is explained by the determinants of the physical conditions of production and real wages.

[15] Or, more exactly, 'would have been (S/C) if Marx had considered complete post-payment of wages'.

174

Now post-multiply both sides of (22) and of (23) by the real wage bundle, w; remembering that $p \cdot w = L = V + S$ in Marx's notation, one obtains

$$V + S = V + rpHw \tag{24}$$

and

$$V + S = (1 + r)V + rpHw, \tag{25}$$

respectively, since $l \cdot w = V$. Thus

$$r = \left(\frac{S}{pHw}\right),$$

from (24) and

$$r = \left(\frac{S}{pHw + V}\right),$$

from (25). Comparing these results with Marx's formulae, one sees that if S is not zero then, whether wages are paid *ex ante* or *ex post*, Marx's formula (S/C) or (S/C + V), is equal to the actual rate of profit r if and only if

$$C = pHw. \tag{26}$$

In words, (26) says that, if S is not zero, Marx's formula for the rate of profit happens to be correct if and only if the labour *embodied* in *all* the capital goods[16] is equal to the labour *commanded* by the capital goods used, directly and indirectly, in producing the wage bundle.[17]

---

[16] 'Capital goods' here *exclude* wage goods, whether or not wages are advanced.

[17] In his paper, 'Profits and Surplus-Value: Appearance and Reality in Capitalist Production', (in E. K. Hunt and J. G. Schwartz (eds.), *A Critique of Economic Theory*, Harmondsworth, 1972), A. Medio has shown that, with wages advanced, $r = [(S/V)/(1 + \omega^*)]$, where ω^* is an appropriately defined 'average value composition' of capital. It will be clear both that Medio's $\omega^* \equiv [(pHw)/V]$ and that his (perfectly correct) result does *nothing* to vindicate Marx's approach to the determination of the profit rate. The average

Relation (26) can, of course, be satisfied but in general it will not be. It was seen in chapter 8[18] that the bundle of commodities appropriated by the capitalists, C, must satisfy

$$l \cdot C = L - l \cdot w \qquad (27)$$

Relation (26) requires that

$$l\mathrm{H}(C + w) = p\mathrm{H}w$$

or

$$l\mathrm{H}C = (p - l)\mathrm{H}w. \qquad (28)$$

For given w, l, H and L ($= 1$), p is determined and thus (27) and (28) are two (hyper-) planes constraining the commodity bundle C. If and only if C lies on their 'intersection' will Marx's formula for the rate of profit happen to give the correct result (with S not zero). Marx's formula is correct only by a fluke and is thus of no interest.

Variations within the labour process

It was seen in chapter 6 that changes within the labour process, such as variations in hours and intensity of work, in pressure to save materials and so on, have their effect on the rate of profit by changing the physical conditions of production which, together with the real wage, are its proximate determinants. The same point will be made again here within the present rather more general framework, though it will still not be possible to draw simple, straightforward conclusions in other than very special cases. This, it must be noted, derives from the inherent complexity of the issues at hand; it must

---

composition ω^* can only be determined by *derivation* from the physical data expressing the conditions of production and real wages, which themselves suffice to determine the rate of profit. In other words, Medio's (perfectly sound) formula is simply a particular formulation of the physical quantities determination of r - it must not be misinterpreted to mean that Marx's approach was 'essentially' correct.

[18] *Cf.*, relation (25) of that chapter, bearing in mind that L = 1, by choice of units, in the present discussion.

176

not be used as an (irrational) excuse for denying the central argument of this book and for 'reverting' to emphasis on value magnitudes, a move which would not overcome the difficulties involved but merely obscure them.

Suppose now then that the 'annual' real wage bundle is fixed, at w, but that the yearly hours of work, the intensity of work and so on are variable. Let A and B now represent the inputs used up in and the outputs produced in the various productive processes over the course of a year. If wages are paid at the end of the year, if workers do no saving and if i is a $(1 \times n)$ row vector of unit elements, then the rate of profit, r, will be determined by

$$i[B - (1+r)A]^{-1}w = 1. \tag{29}$$

Starting from any initial values of A and B, let there be a $100k_j \%$ overall increase in hours and/or intensity in process j,[19] with the result that each element in the jth columns of A and B increases by $100k_j \%$. Then if $\hat{k}$ is the diagonal matrix with the k_j elements along its principal diagonal, (29) will be replaced by

$$i[B(I+\hat{k}) - (1+r)A(I+\hat{k})]^{-1}w = 1,$$

or

$$i(I+\hat{k})^{-1}[B - (1+r)A]^{-1}w = 1. \tag{30}$$

Provided that $[B - (1+r)A]^{-1}w$ is an increasing (vector) function of r, relation (30) will certainly yield a higher value of r than will (29), given the assumption that all the k_j are positive, so that the rate of profit is positively related, for a given real wage, to overall hours and intensity of work.[20]

It will be clear from (30) that if all the k_j were equal, then the effect of the overall increase, of $100k \%$, in hours and/or intensity

[19] Of course, if k_j varies too greatly between processes then some capitalists might eventually lose workers. All the k_j are assumed to be positive.
[20] Of course, if all the k_j were negative, then r would be smaller in (30) than in (29), if $[B - (1+r)A]^{-1}w$ increases in r. (If some k_j were positive and some negative, then the effect on r would not be determinate *a priori*.)

of work would be equivalent, as far as the rate of profit is concerned, to the effect of a $100k\%$ real wage cut, as was seen in chapter 6. When the various k_j are different, however, no such simple equivalence can be established.

It need hardly be said that the above formalization of the effect on the profit rate of overall increases in hours and/or intensity of work is highly simplified. In particular, an increase in, say, the hours worked per year operating process j, while it might well lead to an equal percentage increase in the use of 'current' inputs and in the flow of (normally defined) products, would often not involve any increase in the use of fixed capital inputs or, consequently, in the 'one year older' fixed capital 'products'. Thus *some* of the elements in the jth columns of A and B would be increased but others would not. Similar reasons make it inappropriate to attempt any *simple* generalization of the analysis of chapter 6 in which material inputs were decreased and outputs increased; in the present, more complex framework, a decrease in the use of, say, 2-year old machines as inputs *entails* a decrease in the 'output' of 3-year old machines – the input and output quantities are more tightly linked together once fixed capital is introduced.[21]

That the effects of changes in the labour process on the rate of profit cannot be adequately analysed in a *simple* way does not, of course, mean that they cannot be analysed at all. If they are to affect the rate of profit, changes within the labour process must cause changes in the elements of B and A in (29), w being assumed constant.[22] No matter how different the proportional changes in the elements of, say, the jth columns of A and B might be, the effects of those changes on r can be adequately captured only by the appro-

[21] A further complication is that changes in the economic life of a machine, resulting from, say, changes in the intensity of its utilization, are represented by changes in the *number* of commodities in the system, since differently aged machines are treated as different commodities. It is not, of course, surprising that this should arise as a problem here, since the choice of the best economic life of a machine is a special case of the choice of production method, an issue deliberately ignored in this chapter and to be taken up in the following one.

[22] Or, in more complex cases still, they must cause changes in B, A *and* w.

178

priate, detailed analysis of relation (29) or some other equivalent relation. If such analysis is complex and unlikely to yield many simple *a priori* conclusions, that is no fault in the method of analysis here recommended but is simply the result of the complexity of the phenomena in question. That complexity *cannot* be avoided – whether by reference to (irrelevant) value magnitudes or by any other alleged panacea.

Heterogeneous labour

It was seen in equation (14) of chapter 8 that, in a single-product, circulating capital system, the relation between the rate of profit, r, the vector of money prices, p^m, and the level of the wage rate, w_i, for each of N types of labour, may be written as

$$p^m = (1+r)p^m[A + \Sigma_1^N w_i(w_i \cdot a_i)],\qquad(31)$$

where all wages are paid in advance and A, w_i and a_i are in our usual notation. If now we consider a more general fixed capital using and/or pure joint product producing system, (31) must be replaced by

$$p^m B = (1+r)p^m[A + \Sigma_1^N w_i(w_i \cdot a_i)].\qquad(32)$$

If the row vector of direct and indirect labour requirements of type i labour is defined by $l_i = a_i(B-A)^{-1}$, then (32) can be rewritten[23] as

$$p^m = p^m[rH + (1+r)\Sigma_1^N w_i(w_i \cdot l_i)]\qquad(33)$$

If the matrix on the right of (33) is semi-positive and irreducible, it follows that

$$\lambda^{PF}[rH + (1+r)\Sigma_1^N w_i(w_i \cdot l_i)] = 1\qquad(34)$$

and that $\lambda^{PF}[\cdot]$ is an increasing function of r and of each w_i. For given values of the w_i such that (34) has a positive solution in r, the

[23] Subtract $p^m A$ from both sides of (32) and then post-multiply throughout by $(B-A)^{-1}$.

rate of profit will thus be determined. Relation (34) also implies, of course, that for any given value of r and of any $(N-2)$ w_i, the remaining two w_i values are inversely related, so that *other things being equal*, the real wage levels for different types of labour are in conflict.[24]

Maintaining the assumption that the matrix on the right of (33) is semi-positive and irreducible, it may now be asked what is the condition for the existence of a positive profit rate. Since $\lambda^{PF}[\cdot]$ is increasing in r, it is that

$$\lambda^{PF}[\Sigma_1^N w_i(w_i \cdot l_i)] < 1. \tag{35}$$

But (35) can be shown to be equivalent to

$$\lambda^{PF}(L \cdot W \cdot \hat{w}) < 1, \tag{36}$$

where the ith row of L is l_i, the jth column of W is w_j and $\hat{w}$ is a diagonal matrix with w_j as the jth element along the principal diagonal. Relation (36) is, of course, no more than a variant of relation (10) of chapter 7, the only 'difference' being that the level of each wage rate is here explicitly distinguished from its composition. With only one kind of labour (36) would, of course, collapse to

$$w(l \cdot w) < 1$$

or

$$e > 0,$$

where e is the rate of exploitation. Thus condition (36) is the generalization to the case of many kinds of labour of the condition that, with homogeneous labour, the rate of profit will be positive only if *the* rate of exploitation is positive.[25]

---

[24] If $[rH + (1+r)\Sigma_1^N w_i(w_i \cdot l_i)]$ is not semi-positive or is reducible then, as was noted in the text above, only rather weaker conclusions may be drawn.

[25] It may be noted that a necessary condition for the satisfaction of (36) is that the minimum row sum of $(L \cdot W \cdot \hat{w})$ should be less than unity. Thus if every type of labour is required, directly or indirectly, in the production of at least one wage bundle other than its own, a *necessary* condition for the satisfaction of (36) is that $w_j(l_j \cdot w_j) < 1$ for every j. *Cf.*, the discussion of chapter 7.

Differential profit rates

Since differential wage rates have just been discussed it may be of interest to indicate also how a non-uniform system of profit rates may be analysed. In order to focus attention on this one issue, all labour will now be assumed to obtain the same real wage bundle, denoted by w; it will be readily apparent how the analyses of differential wage rates and differential profit rates may be combined. If the money wage is m and $\hat{r}$ is a diagonal matrix of the profit rates obtained from the operation of the various productive processes then, with wages paid *ex post*,

$$p^m B = ma + p^m A(I + \hat{r}), \tag{37}$$

in our usual notation. From (37), subtracting $p^m A$ from both sides and post-multiplying by $(B - A)^{-1}$,

$$p^m = ml + p^m A\hat{r}(B - A)^{-1}. \tag{38}$$

Now since $p^m \cdot w = m = mL$, (38) implies both that

$$l[I - A\hat{r}(B - A)^{-1}]^{-1}w = L \tag{39}$$

and that

$$p^m = p^m[w \cdot l + A\hat{r}(B - A)^{-1}]. \tag{40}$$

Relation (39) is clearly a simple generalization of (16) above; *provided that* the left-hand side of (39) is an increasing function of every element of $\hat{r}$, it follows that the profit rate in any industry is inversely related to that in every other industry. 'Alternatively', *if* the matrix on the right of (40) is semi-positive and irreducible then

$$\lambda^{PF}[w \cdot l + A\hat{r}(B - A)^{-1}] = 1, \tag{41}$$

where $\lambda^{PF}[\cdot]$ is an increasing function of every element of $\hat{r}$, so that those elements (profit rates) are all inversely related one to another.

While it would be inappropriate here to enter a proper discussion of all the complexities of oligopolistic and monopolistic sectors in the capitalist economy, it may be of interest to note that the result of the previous paragraph is fully in accord with Sweezy's statement that, with given real wages,

'the extra profit of the monopolist comes primarily from the pockets of his fellow capitalists. . . . The tendency to an equality of profit rates which is a characteristic feature of competitive capitalism is thus doubly disrupted by monopoly: the profits of some are raised, while the profits of others are reduced.'[26]

Thus if, in (39) or (41), all the elements of $\hat{r}$ are 'at first' equal but one or more elements 'then' rise *above* that common level, one or more of the other elements of $\hat{r}$ must fall *below* that level. (This is only a *conceptual* comparison, of course: the historical development of monopoly conditions involves many changes in the elements of (39) or (41) other than those referring directly to rates of profit.) It need hardly be said that neither (39) nor (41), nor any equivalent relation, provides a theory of monopoly; such relationships may nonetheless be useful in the analysis of monopoly, by showing exactly how changes in real wages and conditions of production – caused in part by the development of monopoly conditions – limit the possible combinations of profit rates in different productive activities, without reference to any value magnitude.

It may also be noted that if profit rates, even though unequal, exhibit a stable structure in relative terms, then $\hat{r}$ may be written as $r \cdot \bar{r}$, where $\bar{r}$ represents the *relative* magnitudes of profit rates in different processes, while the scalar r represents the 'overall level' of profit rates. Relation (38) then becomes *formally* equivalent to the relation for an economy with a uniform profit rate but can still be used to show how the structure of unequal profit rates will influence prices and the 'overall level' of the profit rate, r.

The turnover of capital
It has already been seen that the joint production framework makes

[26] P. M. Sweezy, *The Theory of Capitalist Development*, London, 1962, p. 273.

possible the proper analysis of the depreciation of fixed capital. Since the latter is a central aspect of the more general issue of the 'turnover of capital' it might be expected that the general joint production framework can be used to analyse other turnover problems, such as the timing of wage payments and the role of circulation activities, both discussed in chapter 8; this is indeed the case.

It was assumed, arbitrarily, at the beginning of this chapter that each productive process takes one 'year' to complete but such a strong assumption is not really necessary. Suppose instead – and far more plausibly – that each process takes an integer multiple of some short period,[27] called a 'week', and that wages are paid at the end of each week. All inputs to and outputs from a 'productive activity' are now defined to be those involved *in one week's operation*; a process which, in the everyday sense, takes several, or many, weeks is thus broken down into a sequence of one-week-long processes. Correspondingly, the number of products involved will be increased, perhaps greatly, since any 'semi-finished' product, in the normal sense, will now appear as one of the specific products of a particular week-long process and must be regarded as a distinct 'commodity'.[28] Each product, whether a finished product, a semi-finished product or a partially used piece of fixed capital equipment is thus treated as a distinct 'commodity' and has its own price of production.[29] Indeed a commodity entering a circulation process is treated as being distinct from the 'same' commodity, in the everyday sense, leaving that process, so that these 'two commodities' will have distinct prices (as was seen in the final section of chapter 8).

[27] There are, of course, continuous flow processes which are not properly represented even under this assumption.
[28] A terminological problem arises here when the term 'commodity' is restricted to a product produced for sale: semi-finished products can perhaps reasonably be regarded as latent, or honorary, 'commodities'.
[29] Obviously another terminological problem may arise at this point: price of production is used here to mean the price of *any* 'commodity' corresponding to a given real wage and a uniform rate of profit.

Once the above conventions have been adopted, one may simply write

$$p^m B = ma + (1+r)p^m A, \qquad (42)$$

where it is now understood that r is the rate of profit per 'week', that B, a and A refer to *all* the week-long production activities and that p^m, B and A contain entries for *every* 'commodity' as now defined. It is apparent that (42) is no different in logical structure from the equivalent relations used throughout this chapter, so that everything said above can be re-said within the new interpretation. The latter, however, implicitly deals with many of the usual problems relating to the turnover of capital, since all the complexities of fixed capital depreciation, differing periods of production, periods of circulation and so on are built into the information contained in A, B and a. The joint production framework thus provides a clear and coherent basis for the analysis of turnover problems, showing how they can be analysed in terms of the physical conditions of production, circulation and real wages, no value magnitudes being of any significance for such analysis.[30]

[30] The points made in this section are discussed more fully in M. Morishima, *Theory of Economic Growth*, Oxford, 1969, chapter VI and the same author's *Marx's Economics*, Cambridge, 1973, chapter 13.

13

The Determination of Labour Allocation

In chapter 12, as in most of the preceding chapters, the patterns of output, of labour allocation and of choice of production methods were taken as given. It will now be considered, at a high level of abstraction, how labour allocation, etc., is determined in an abstract capitalist economy. It will also be shown how the existence of positive profit can be linked to the existence of positive surplus labour, even in the presence of fixed capital and/or pure joint products, provided that Marx's concept of additive values is abandoned. The analyses will be presented first in terms of a simple numerical example and then, very briefly, in a general form.[1]

The choice of production methods

It was seen in chapter 4 that, with no fixed capital and no pure joint products, the choice of production methods is simple to analyse. If there are constant returns to scale and if wages are paid in advance,[2] then in that simple context any chosen combination of one production method for each product, combination j, will be represented by

---

[1] The analyses presented here are entirely unoriginal. The reader familiar with both J. von Neumann, 'A Model of General Economic Equilibrium', *Review of Economic Studies*, 1945–6 and M. Morishima, 'Marx in the Light of Modern Economic Theory', *Econometrica*, 1974, will find little of interest in this chapter, unless it be in the concluding sections.

[2] Both assumptions will be made throughout this chapter, the former being essential to the argument, the latter merely a convenience.

an input matrix, A_j^+, which includes the real wage bundle advanced, and will imply a rate of profit, r_j, given by

$$(1 + r_j)^{-1} = \lambda^{PF}(A_j^+).$$

Competitive forces will lead to the choice of that combination of methods of production which simultaneously yields the highest rate of profit and minimizes the money price of every commodity relative to the money wage. Two features of this determination of the choice of technique in a single product, circulating capital system may be noted. First, since each process produces only one product, no product can possibly have a zero price, for such a price would entail the existence of an industry with zero revenue. Second, with constant returns to scale, the set of production methods chosen is independent of the pattern of output and of the social allocation of labour. Different output patterns will, of course, imply different relative sizes of the various industries, and thus different allocations of labour, but they will not affect *which* production methods are used.

The situation is more complex, however, once fixed capital and/or pure joint products are allowed for. If any particular process produces more than one product, then one (or perhaps more) of those products could have a zero price, without thereby giving a zero revenue from that process. For example, a zero price for the waste mud produced is quite consistent with the existence of positive revenue in the cement making industry. Again, a number of processes producing the same 'product' in the ordinary sense but using (otherwise similar) machines of different ages will be such that all but one of them will have two products with a positive price ('the' product and an old but still valuable machine), while the remaining process will have only one positively priced product, the about-to-be-scrapped machine having a zero price. Thus, with joint production, zero prices are possible for some 'products'. It is also the case that, even with constant returns to scale, the joint production methods used may depend on the pattern of output. Thus, both because some prices can be zero and because the choice of production methods may depend on what is being produced, the analysis of the choice of method, and hence the social allocation of labour, is more complex once joint production is allowed for, as it must be if an adequate analysis of the capitalist economy is to be achieved. The most powerful analysis available of a capitalist, joint production economy is that due to von Neumann, cited above;[3] before presenting a more general version of his argument, however, it will be used in a further examination of the simple numerical example of chapter 11, which will also be used to illustrate Morishima's analysis of surplus labour in a joint production system.

A simple example

In the example used in chapter 11, the inputs to and the outputs from the two available processes, when operated by one unit of labour, were given by the A and B matrices:[4]

$$A = \begin{bmatrix} 5 & 0 \\ 0 & 10 \end{bmatrix},$$

$$B = \begin{bmatrix} 6 & 3 \\ 1 & 12 \end{bmatrix}, \tag{1}$$

where, in both A and B, the first row referred to commodity 1 and the second to commodity 2. The real wage bundle was taken to be (3, 5) for every six units of labour-time, or (1/2, 5/6) for each unit. Thus, if wages are now assumed to be advanced,[5] the matrix A^+, including both the material inputs *and* the real wages required when one unit of labour-time is used, is given by

$$A^+ = \begin{bmatrix} 5\tfrac{1}{2} & \tfrac{1}{2} \\ \tfrac{5}{6} & 10\tfrac{5}{6} \end{bmatrix} \tag{2}$$

Suppose now that x_1 units of labour-time are used to operate the

[3] See footnote 1.
[4] Note that processes are here portrayed in the *columns* of A and B, whereas they appeared in the *rows* of Table I, chapter 11.
[5] They were taken to be paid *ex post* in chapter 11.

first process and x_2 units to operate the second. From (2), the total commodity stocks required at the beginning of the production period will be

$$5\tfrac{1}{2}x_1 + \tfrac{1}{2}x_2, \tag{3}$$

for commodity 1 and

$$\tfrac{5}{6}x_1 + 10\tfrac{5}{6}x_2, \tag{4}$$

for commodity 2.

From B in (1), the commodity outputs at the end of the production period will be

$$6x_1 + 3x_2, \tag{5}$$

for commodity 1 and

$$x_1 + 12x_2, \tag{6}$$

for commodity 2. Now if workers do no saving, as assumed here, then if capitalists reinvest all their profits, so that no 'surplus product' is consumed (as will also be assumed), the output of each commodity at the end of the period will be available for use as commodity input at the beginning of the next period. Let $100g$ be the maximum percentage rate at which the input – and the output – of each commodity can grow. From (3) and (5) it is seen that, for commodity 1,

$$(1+g)(5\tfrac{1}{2}x_1 + \tfrac{1}{2}x_2) \leqq (6x_1 + 3x_2), \tag{7}$$

while for commodity 2 it follows from (4) and (6) that

$$(1+g)(\tfrac{5}{6}x_1 + 10\tfrac{5}{6}x_2) \leqq (x_1 + 12x_2). \tag{8}$$

Relation (7) states that, in a given production period, the total output of commodity 1 is at least $(1+g)$ times the total input of commodity 1 (both as material input and as real wages); relation (8) makes the analogous statement for commodity 2. von Neumann now imposes the (reasonable) rule that if, say, relation (7) is satisfied with *strict inequality*, so that more commodity 1 is produced each period than is used as input in the following period, then commodity 1 will have a zero price ($p_1 = 0$). Again, if relation (8) is satisfied with strict inequality, then $p_2 = 0$. Consequently, whether (7) and (8) are equalities or inequalities, we have:

$$(1+g)(5\tfrac{1}{2}x_1 + \tfrac{1}{2}x_2)p_1 = (6x_1 + 3x_2)p_1 \qquad (9)$$

and

$$(1+g)(\tfrac{5}{6}x_1 + 10\tfrac{5}{6}x_2)p_2 = (x_1 + 12x_2)p_2. \qquad (10)$$

If (7) is an equality then (9) holds whether p_1 is positive or zero; if (7) is an inequality then (9) holds because p_1 is zero – and similarly for (8) and (10).

Now let r be the rate of profit; if, at the prices of production p_1 and p_2, a process can yield that rate of profit it may be used but if it cannot yield profit at the rate r then it will not be used. Thus reading down the columns of A^+ and B, one finds that

$$(1+r)(5\tfrac{1}{2}p_1 + \tfrac{5}{6}p_2) \geqq (6p_1 + p_2), \qquad (11)$$

for the first process and

$$(1+r)(\tfrac{1}{2}p_1 + 10\tfrac{5}{6}p_2) \geqq (3p_1 + 12p_2), \qquad (12)$$

for the second. Relation (11) states that the total revenue from the output of process one, operated by one unit of labour, will be less than or equal to $(1+r)$ times the total cost of the inputs; relation (12) refers similarly to process two. Thus if r_1 be the rate of profit which would be obtained on process one if it were operated, where $(1+r_1) \equiv (6p_1 + p_2)/(5\tfrac{1}{2}p_1 + \tfrac{5}{6}p_2)$, relation (11) states that $(1+r) \geqq (1+r_1)$; in the same way, relation (12) states that $(1+r) \geqq (1+r_2)$, where $(1+r_2) \equiv (3p_1 + 12p_2)/(\tfrac{1}{2}p_1 + 10\tfrac{5}{6}p_2)$. Now consider the equalities

$$(1+r)(5\tfrac{1}{2}p_1 + \tfrac{5}{6}p_2)x_1 = (6p_1 + p_2)x_1 \qquad (13)$$

and

$$(1+r)(\tfrac{1}{2}p_1 + 10\tfrac{5}{6}p_2)x_2 = (3p_1 + 12p_2)x_2. \qquad (14)$$

Relation (13) guarantees that if (11) is a *strict inequality*, and thus process one does not yield the profit rate r, then $x_1 = 0$, i.e., process one is not used. In the same way, (12) and (14) show that process two is not used if it cannot yield the profit rate r.

von Neumann's question is then whether there exist non-negative values of x_1, x_2, p_1 and p_2 such that (7)–(14) are all satisfied, with $(1+r)$ and $(1+g)$ positive. If such values exist, then it will have been shown how the rates of profit and of growth, the allocation of labour, the patterns of inputs and outputs and commodity prices are determined, in an abstract capitalist economy, by the available methods of production, the real wage bundle and the capitalists' drive to accumulate.

While the equivalent existence proof is far from trivial in the general case, in the present example it is easy to show that (7)–(14) are satisfied by

$$r = g = \left[\frac{29+9\sqrt{6}}{3.55}\right]\% \doteq 14.37\% \tag{15}$$

$$x_1 = (1+3\sqrt{6})x_2 \doteq 8.347x_2 \tag{16}$$

$$p_1 = \left[\frac{\sqrt{6}-1}{9}\right]p_2 \doteq 0.161p_2 \tag{17}$$

A number of features of this solution may be noted. First, from (15), the rates of profit and growth are equal – as will be seen below this is a general result – and are less than the rates of 20% obtained in chapter 11. This lower rate results, of course, from the wages here being advanced.[6] Second, from (16), both x_1 and x_2 are positive, so that both processes are used, but only their ratio, and not their absolute magnitudes, are determined: this is of course to be expected in a steadily expanding system. Third, from (17), both commodities

---

[6] It may be noted that, since the additive value calculations of chapter 11 were independent of the pre- or post-payment of wages, it has now been shown (implicitly) that the previous finding that positive profits could co-exist with negative, additively defined surplus value did not depend on wages not being advanced.

are positively priced, so that neither is produced in excess of requirements, but only relative prices are determined, which is to be
expected in an analysis not treating money explicitly.

That the solution of a von Neumann analysis need not involve
that all processes are used or that all products have a positive price
may be seen by modifying the above example. Suppose now that the
real wage bundle per unit of labour-time is (w_1, w_2), where $1 < w_1
< 3$ and $1 < w_2 < 2$. The input matrix will now be

$$A^+ = \begin{bmatrix} 5+w_1 & w_1 \\ w_2 & 10+w_2 \end{bmatrix} \tag{18}$$

From (1) and (18), the profitability condition for process one,
corresponding to (11) above, will now be

$$(1+r)[(5+w_1)p_1 + w_2p_2] \geqq 6p_1 + p_2$$

or

$$r[(5+w_1)p_1 + w_2p_2] \geqq (1-w_1)p_1 + (1-w_2)p_2. \tag{19}$$

With w_1 and w_2 both greater than unity, (19) could be satisfied as
an equality, at non-negative prices, only for the prices $p_1 = p_2 = 0$.
But it is economically meaningless for *all* produced commodities to
have zero prices in a growth equilibrium, so that in any meaningful
case (19) must be satisfied as a strict inequality. Thus process one
will not be used ($x_1 = 0$). Setting $x_2 = 1$ (process two must be used
if there is to be an economy to examine!), we now have

$$(1+g)w_1 \leqq 3 \tag{7'}$$

$$(1+g)(10+w_2) \leqq 12 \tag{8'}$$

$$(1+g)w_1p_1 = 3p_1 \tag{9'}$$

$$(1+g)(10+w_2)p_2 = 12p_2 \tag{10'}$$

$$(1+r)[w_1p_1 + (10+w_2)p_2] = (3p_1 + 12p_2) \tag{14'}$$

where (7'), etc. correspond to and are to be interpreted in the same
way as (7), etc. above. Comparing the sum of (9') and (10') with

(14'), and remembering that p_1 and p_2 cannot both be zero, one sees that $r = g$.

Comparing (7') and (8'), one finds that *if*

$$(10 + w_2) = 4w_1$$

then *both* relations will be satisfied with equality, so that

$$r = g = \left[\frac{3 - w_1}{w_1} \right] = \left[\frac{2 - w_2}{10 + w_2} \right] \qquad (20)$$

and both commodities *can* have a positive price. They need not do so however. With $(10 + w_2) = 4w_1$, the single process in use *both uses and produces* the two commodities in the proportions one to four, so that there is, in effect, a single 'composite commodity', the relative prices of its components being *indeterminate*.

The exact satisfaction of $(10 + w_2) = 4w_1$ is, however, a somewhat marginal case. If $(10 + w_2) < 4w_1$ then only (7') can be an equality, (8') being a strict inequality, so that $r = g = [(3 - w_1)/w_1]$ and commodity 2 is 'over-produced', with $p_2 = 0$. If, on the other hand, $(10 + w_2) > 4w_1$, then (8') becomes an equality and (7') a strict inequality, so that $r = g = [(2 - w_2)/(10 + w_2)]$ and commodity 1 is 'over-produced', with $p_1 = 0$.

The various simple cases above thus illustrate the general point that, in a von Neumann analysis of a joint production system, there may or may not be some available processes which are not used and there may or may not be some products with a zero price. Even with given available methods, the choice of method(s) and which product(s) have zero prices may depend upon the level and composition of the real wage bundle. It is also possible that relative commodity prices should not be fully determinate; the same is true, in general, of relative process employment levels, though that is not, of course, illustrated above. The rates of profit and of accumulation are, however, fully determined[7] and *are equal* to one another.

---

[7] See below for the assumptions needed to ensure uniqueness of the rate of profit/accumulation.

Morishima's analysis of surplus labour

It was seen in chapter 11 that the above numerical example, with a real wage bundle of $(\frac{1}{2}, \frac{5}{6})$, yields a *negative* 'surplus value', where the latter is calculated in terms of *additive* values, even though profits and prices are positive. In the work cited above,[8] Morishima has proposed an interpretation of necessary and surplus labour which is such that profits will be positive if and only if surplus labour, as defined by Morishima, is positive. This approach will now be illustrated in terms of the numerical example of chapter 11; the analysis is the same whether wages are paid *ex ante* or *ex post*.

Let the real wage bundle for 6 units of labour-time be (3, 5) as before. We now ask what is the smallest amount of labour-time required for the production of that commodity bundle, given the *available* methods of production. (It is to be noted that attention is *not* confined to the processes *actually used* by capitalists, which will generally be only a sub-set of the available processes, of course.)[9] That amount of labour-time will be Morishima's 'necessary' labour-time and the difference between total labour, 6, and this 'necessary' labour-time will, by definition, be Morishima's 'surplus' labour.

Let x_1 and x_2 be the amounts of labour-time allocated to processes one and two respectively. As may be seen from (1), the matrix of *net* outputs, per unit of labour-time, C, is given by

$$(B - A) = C = \begin{bmatrix} 1 & 3 \\ 1 & 2 \end{bmatrix}. \qquad (21)$$

It is thus required that

$$x_1 + 3x_2 \geqq 3, \text{ for commodity 1 and}$$

$$x_1 + 2x_2 \geqq 5, \text{ for commodity 2.}$$

---

[8] See footnote 1.

[9] In the present example capitalists *do* use all the available processes when the wage bundle is (3, 5) for every 6 units of labour-time but that is merely a special property of this particular numerical example.

Total labour-time will be $(x_1 + x_2)$, so that the formal problem is to

$$\text{Minimize} \quad V = x_1 + x_2$$

$$\text{subject to} \begin{cases} x_1 + 3x_2 \geq 3 & (22) \\ x_1 + 2x_2 \geq 5 & (23) \\ x_1, x_2 \geq 0 & (24)^{10} \end{cases}$$

Now, denoting the solution values for this problem by asterisks, it is easy to show that V is minimized, subject to the conditions (22)–(24), when $x_1{}^* = 0$, $x_2{}^* = 2\frac{1}{2}$, $V^* = 2\frac{1}{2}$. In words, the labour-time minimizing way of producing the wage bundle (3, 5) is not to use process one at all and to allocate $2\frac{1}{2}$ units of labour-time to process two. As may be seen from the second column of C in (21), the net product will then be $(7\frac{1}{2}, 5)$, which is equal to the wage bundle (3, 5) *plus* $4\frac{1}{2}$ units of commodity 1. Commodity 1 is thus 'over-produced' but this is still the 'cheapest' way, in terms of labour-time, to produce the wage bundle.[11] Necessary labour being $2\frac{1}{2}$, for the production of the wage bundle going to 6 units of labour-time, Morishima's surplus labour, S^*, is given by $S^* = 6 - 2\frac{1}{2} = 3\frac{1}{2}$. His rate of exploitation is then $e^* \equiv (S^*/V^*) = (3.5/2.5) = 140\%$.[12] The (newly defined) rate of exploitation, like the rate of profit, is positive.

It will naturally be clear that this result is perfectly consistent with that found in chapter 11, for the definitions of surplus and of the rate of exploitation used are quite different. It may well be thought, however, that of the two approaches Morishima's should be the more congenial to Marxist economists. It provides a clear and

[10] To be economically meaningful, the labour-time allocations x_1 and x_2 must both be non-negative.

[11] Disposal of the 'surplus' units of commodity 1 is assumed to be costless.

[12] These figures were given in earlier versions of my paper 'Positive Profits with Negative Surplus Value' but were omitted from the version published in the *Economic Journal*, 1975, in order to save space. They were subsequently published in M. Morishima, 'Positive Profits with Negative Surplus Value: A Comment', *Economic Journal*, 1976.

194

meaningful definition of necessary labour, surplus labour and the
rate of exploitation which, even in the context of a general joint
production system,[13] can be used to show that the rate of profit will
be positive if and only if the (newly defined) rate of exploitation is
positive.[14] It has to be noted, however, that the determination of
Morishima's necessary and surplus labour quantities requires
knowledge only of the physical conditions of production and real
wages; no reference whatever is made to Marx's additive values.
Morishima's approach thus fits in well with the orientation of the
present work: traditional Marxist value magnitudes have nothing to
contribute to the analysis of the rate of profit, of production prices
or even, in the fixed capital/joint products context, to the analysis of
surplus labour and its connection with positive profits. On the other
hand, all those matters can be analysed in terms of physically
specified conditions of production and real wages.

The general case
The von Neumann and Morishima analyses illustrated above will
now be presented in their general form, albeit briefly and without
proofs of the results. It will be recalled from the final section of the
previous chapter that it is convenient to assume that every real
production or circulation activity takes an integer multiple of some
(probably short) period, called a 'week', and can thus be analysed
into a succession of one-week-long activities. Correspondingly,
anything which is an input to or an output from any week-long
process is treated as a distinct 'commodity' with its own 'price of
production'. It will be assumed here that wages are advanced.
    Whereas the commodities produced and the processes actually

[13] In a single product, circulating capital system Morishima's approach will
yield the same measure of surplus labour as will the additive value accounts –
though without any need to calculate individual commodity values – *if* the
processes actually used by the capitalists are those adopted in the labour-time
minimizing allocation (which in general they will not be).
[14] See below.

used were assumed to be known and equal in number in the last chapter, so that the A and B matrices were both square, we now need to represent the inputs to and the outputs from every *available* process of production, since one aim of the analysis is precisely to determine which processes are used and which not. Thus, in this chapter A and B, the jth columns of which will represent the inputs to and the outputs from the jth process when it is operated by one unit of labour-time,[15] must be assumed to be rectangular. (In each matrix the number of rows is the number of 'commodities' as now defined, while the number of columns is the number of *available* processes.) If the real wage bundle is the column vector w per unit of labour-time and i is a row vector of unit elements with as many elements as there are processes, then

$$A^+ \equiv A + w \cdot i$$

is the matrix of inputs *including* real wages, as before.

Now let x be the semi-positive column vector showing how much labour-time is allocated to each process; if $x_j = 0$ then process j is not used. Let p be the semi-positive row vector representing the production prices of the various 'products'; if $p_i = 0$ then product i is not an 'economic good' (not a 'commodity'). (One important class of products with zero prices is, of course, the set of about-to-be-scrapped machines.) Finally, let g and r be the growth rate and the profit rate, respectively.

Assuming, as above, that workers do not save, while capitalists reinvest all their profits, the growth rate g is constrained by

$$(1 + g)A^+ x \leqq Bx; \tag{25}$$

the output of each commodity at the end of a 'week' must be at least $(1 + g)$ times the input of that commodity at the beginning of the 'week'. The stipulation that any product produced 'in excess of

[15] It is, of course, implicit in this normalization that labour is used in every week-long process. This assumption, whilst not essential, has the advantage that the 'process intensity' vector x can now be interpreted directly as the labour allocation vector – see below.

196

replacement and growth requirements' should have a zero price can, from (25), be represented by the condition

$$(1+g)p\mathbf{A}^+x = p\mathbf{B}x. \tag{26}$$

Since no process can yield more than the profit rate r, we have

$$(1+r)p\mathbf{A}^+ \geqq p\mathbf{B}; \tag{27}$$

the revenue from any process is at most equal to $(1+r)$ times the capital advanced to set it in motion. Of course if (27) should hold as a strict inequality for process j then $x_j = 0$, which can be expressed by the condition

$$(1+r)p\mathbf{A}^+x = p\mathbf{B}x. \tag{28}$$

A proof that (25)–(28) can be satisfied by semi-positive x and p and by positive $(1+g)$, $(1+r)$, for economically meaningful $\mathbf{A}^+$ and $\mathbf{B}$, will not be given here but a number of points may be noted. First, from (26) and (28),

$$(1+g)p\mathbf{A}^+x = (1+r)p\mathbf{A}^+x = p\mathbf{B}x.$$

Thus either $r = g$ or $p\mathbf{A}^+x = p\mathbf{B}x = 0$; but the second 'solution', with zero total capital and output, cannot characterize a meaningful economic system, so leaving it aside, we have

$$r = g.$$

The rates of profit and growth must be equal. Second, if any 'solutions' to (25)–(28) involving a zero total wage bill are ignored, the value of $r = g$ is uniquely determined.[16] On the other hand, the labour allocation and price vectors, x and p, may or may not be uniquely determined. (That x may not be uniquely determined is to be expected from our analysis of choice of technique in chapter 4; if the solution value of $r = g$ should be a 'switch-point' value, then

---

[16] See T. Fujimoto, 'Duality and the Uniqueness of Growth Equilibrium', *International Economic Review*, 1975 and M. Morishima, 'Marx from a von Neumann Viewpoint' (in) M. Brown, K. Sato and P. Zarembka (eds.), *Essays in Modern Capital Theory*, Amsterdam, 1976.

alternative method choices are equally profitable, so that the social allocation of labour between processes is not fully determined by the analysis.)

Thus, on the basis of the physically specified *available* methods of production and circulation and the real wage bundle, together with the assumptions that capitalists accumulate all their profits, that 'over-produced' products are zero-priced and that competitive conditions prevail,[17] the von Neumann analysis can be used to show that the rates of profit and growth are equal and uniquely determined[18] and to 'determine' (though perhaps not uniquely) the social allocation of labour-time and the 'production prices' of all 'commodities'. No reference whatsoever is made to *any* embodied labour-time magnitude.

The 'law of value'

The term 'law of value' is used with more than one meaning but its general thrust is perhaps well captured in the following statement by Mandel:

'In Marxist economic theory, the "law of value" fulfils a triple function. In the first place it . . . establishes the *axis* around which *long-term changes* in relative prices of commodities oscillate. . . . In the second place it determines the relative proportions of total social

---

[17] One can still read such statements as the following: 'All modern "price theory" . . . derives from the category "utility" or the relationship between "wealth" . . . and the "individual consumer".' (G. Pilling, 'The Law of Value in Ricardo and Marx', *Economy and Society*, 1973, p. 39.) Such statements are amazingly ignorant – *much* modern academic economics starts from the von Neumann basis of objective data and makes *no* reference to 'utility'. Marx's sharp criticisms of classical and vulgar political economy were based on a deep and extensive *knowledge* of their real content; would-be critics of contemporary academic economics should follow his example in this respect. They will still find much to criticize, there being no 'need' to invent such fairy stories as that due to Pilling, just quoted.

[18] It can also be shown that $r = g$ is inversely related to the level of the real wage bundle; see, for example, the works cited in footnote 16.

labour . . . devoted to the output of different groups of commodities. . . . In the third place it rules economic growth, by determining the average rate of profit. . . .'[19]

The von Neumann analysis determines the rates of profit and of accumulation and also 'determines' the production prices of commodities and the social allocation of labour, i.e. it does all that the 'law of value' is supposed to do according to Mandel. Yet it does this without reference to any Marxist value magnitude.[20]

Morishima's analysis

In terms of our above notation and assumptions, Morishima's analysis of surplus labour may be presented as follows. Let i be a row vector of unit elements with as many elements as there are processes. Then $V = i \cdot x$ is the amount of total labour-time. Consider now the (linear programming) problem:

$$\text{Minimize} \quad V = i \cdot x$$

$$\text{subject to} \quad \begin{cases} Bx \geqq Ax + w \\ x \geqq 0 \end{cases}$$

[19] Introduction to Karl Marx. *Capital*, vol. I, Penguin/NLR edition, 1976, pp. 41–2.

[20] If the solution to (25)−(28) should involve *no* 'overproduction' of *any* product (which is most unlikely, for there are always waste products and machines about to be scrapped) then (25) would become an equality $(1+g)A^+x = Bx$ or $(B-A^+)x = gA^+x$. Since $(B-A^+)x$ is the vector of commodities appropriated by the capitalists and A^+x that of total commodity capital advanced, the *physical* surplus is then strictly proportional to the *physical* capital. It follows that $r = g = [z(B-A^+)x/zA^+x]$ where z is *any* set of semi-positive weights. It therefore follows in turn that $r = g = (S/C+V)$, *whatever* labour values might be (provided that they do not imply $S = C+V = 0$). This, of course, is no vindication of Marx's formula for the rate of profit! If, as is probable, the solution to (25)−(28) involves some 'overproduction', then (25) becomes $(1+g)A^+x+y = Bx$ or $(B-A^+)x = gA^+x +y$, where y is the semi-positive vector of 'surplus' products. Thus $r = g = [z(B-A^+)x/zA^+x]$ if and only if $z \cdot y = 0$, that is, if and only if a zero weight z_j is attached to every product j which is in surplus ($y_j > 0$). As normally interpreted, Marx's additive value accounts will not, in general, yield a value vector z such that $z \cdot y = 0$ (or even such that z is semi-positive), so that $r = g \neq (S/C+V)$, in general, even in a von Neumann solution.

The solution[21] to this problem, x^* and $V^* = i \cdot x^*$, shows the labour allocation which minimizes the total labour-time required to produce a bundle of commodities at least as large as the wage bundle for one unit of labour-time. (There is, of course, no presumption that the same processes will be used in x^* as in the solution vector(s) x which solved (25)–(28) above.) Surplus labour S^* is now given by $S^* = (1 - V^*)$ and the rate of exploitation by $e^* = (S^*/V^*) = [(1 - V^*)/V^*]$. It will be seen that e^* is determined directly and uniquely by A, B and w, no reference to any value magnitudes being required.[22]

Using the e^* definition of exploitation and defining the capacity growth rate as the highest growth rate possible subject to (25) above, Morishima is able to prove that, under certain reasonable assumptions,

'Positive exploitation is necessary and sufficient for the system to have positive growth capacity as well as to guarantee capitalists positive profits.'[23]

Thus, as Morishima points out, the 'three propositions (i) that capitalists exploit workers . . . (ii) that the capitalist system is profitable . . . and (iii) that the capitalist system is productive [able to grow, I.S.] are all equivalent.'[24] The problem then, of course, is

---

[21] x^* need not be unique but V^* necessarily will be.

[22] Of course, the problem Min $V = i \cdot x$, subject to $Bx \geqq Ax + w$, $x \geqq 0$ has a dual, Max $L = v \cdot w$, subject to $vB \leqq vA + i$, $v \geqq 0$; $L^* = V^*$ and the elements of v^* can be interpreted as 'marginal necessary labour costs' of the various commodities. Thus $e^* = (1 - v^* \cdot w/v^* \cdot w)$, which is very similar to the formula $e = (1 - l \cdot w/l \cdot w)$ used repeatedly in earlier chapters. It must be noted carefully, therefore, that v^* is not, in general, related to the methods of production *actually used* in the capitalist economy; nor is it necessarily unique, even though L^* is, of course. Consequently, one cannot identify v^* with Marx's values; e^* is defined by A, B and w and the interpretation of v^* must not be allowed to give the impression that, in the end, Marx's value magnitude analysis is vindicated. (Morishima, it need hardly be said, is perfectly clear on this point: it is to be hoped that others do not attempt to obscure it.)

[23] Morishima, *op. cit.*, (footnote 1) p. 621.

[24] *Ibid.*

to explain *why* A, B and *w* are such that exploitation, profitability and growth capacity exist and continue to exist in a capitalist society.

Conclusion

At a high level of abstraction, the von Neumann analysis, supplemented by Morishima's new definitions of surplus labour and exploitation, shows how the physical conditions of production and circulation and the real wage (i) determine the rates of profit and of accumulation, (ii) 'determine' the social allocation of labour, which production and circulation processes are used, at what age machines, etc. are scrapped, (iii) 'determine' the production prices of all products, including old machines and waste products, (iv) determine the level of (newly defined) surplus labour, which is positive if and only if the rates of profit and accumulation are positive. Marx's value magnitude analysis makes *no* contribution to that demonstration.

It need hardly be said that the von Neumann analysis tells one little or nothing about many very important matters,[25] for example variations within the labour process, technical change more generally considered, the role of money, crises, state economic activity, and

[25] It may be noted, however, that heterogeneous labour can be dealt with in the von Neumann analysis, provided that there is a given real wage bundle for each type of labour and that each type is always available in the required amount. The matrix A^+ simply has to be adjusted to include *all* the real wage components of the capital required to activate each process. (The unit activity level of each process may not now be definable in terms of one unit of some *common* type of labour-time but this is an inessential change.) In an unpublished paper, *The Fundamental Marxian Theorem with Heterogeneous Labour*, Y. Fujimori, of Josai University, has argued that Morishima's result concerning surplus labour, profits and growth can be generalized to include heterogeneous labour. It is also to be noted that the von Neumann analysis can be extended to deal with foreign trade: it follows that Morishima's analysis can be so extended. By contrast, one may ask 'How could the traditional Marxist embodied labour content of commodities be determined in an open economy, when there is no way of allocating to individual commodities, produced with imported means of production, the labour used to produce the exports which 'pay' for those imports?'

so on. Yet this truth, while not to be ignored, must not be made an excuse for denying the very real achievements of such analysis in dealing with questions which were important to Marx and are still important today for anyone concerned to understand capitalist society. The irrelevance of Marx's value magnitudes to the understanding of certain fundamental issues has been conclusively demonstrated. If any wish to argue that it is necessary to the understanding of other important issues, let them *demonstrate* that necessity, clearly and without equivocation, by showing how value quantities (which are mere derivates of the physical conditions) can provide a coherent explanation of such issues, where no other explanation is adequate!

14

Summary Statement and Implications

Sacrificing elegance, I give a sharp statement of the principal propositions which have been obtained above, on the basis of the underlying assumptions set out in chapter 1 and the various more specific assumptions stated at the appropriate points throughout the text, before outlining certain implications which may be drawn from these findings.

I. If there is only one available method for the production of each commodity, each method using only circulating capital and producing only one product then:

i) the physical quantities of commodities and of labour specifying the methods of production, together with the physical quantities of commodities specifying the given real wage rate, suffice to determine the rate of profit (and the associated prices of production);

ii) the labour-time required (directly and indirectly) to produce any commodity – and thus the value of any commodity – is determined by the physical data relating to the methods of production; it follows that value magnitudes are, at best, redundant in the determination of the rate of profit (and prices of production);

iii) the straightforward schema for the determination of the rate of profit (and prices of production) in terms of physical quantities can be converted into a schema of values by the procedure of multiplying each physical quantity of a commodity by its value, while simultaneously dividing the price of that commodity by the same value. Yet this procedure, while possible, is pointless, for it adds *nothing* to one's understanding. The traditional value schema, in which all the constant capital and all the variable capital elements in a productive activity are summed and represented by a single 'c' and a single 'v' figure, is not adequate to the determination of the rate of profit (and prices of production).

II. Under the same conditions as for I above, the rate of profit is positive if and only if surplus labour is positive. This result does not, in itself, constitute an *explanation* of the existence of profit.

III. If the number of available methods of production is equal to the number of commodities and those methods employ fixed capital and/or produce (pure) joint products then:

i) the physical data, referring to production methods and the real wage, still suffice to determine the rate of profit (and prices of production);

ii) the various quantities of embodied labour-time, and thus values, *defined in Marx's additive way*, may be indeterminate. When they are determinate, they can be positive, zero or negative: therefore additive surplus value can be positive, zero or negative;

iii) the existence of (positive) profit is now compatible with positive, zero or negative additive surplus value.

IV. If there are alternative methods of production, no matter how small the number of alternatives, then:

i) the profit maximizing choice of production methods will depend on the given real wage rate – but, for a given wage, the rate of profit and prices of production are still determined by the physical quantities representing the alternative production methods and that real wage;

ii) the amounts of labour-time required for the production of commodities are only determined once the choice of production methods is known. But that choice is made in maximizing the rate of profit.

The determination of the profit rate (and prices of production) is thus logically *prior* to the determination of the values of commodities. Clearly, then, values cannot determine the rate of profit (or the prices of production);

iii) if the real wage rate should be such that alternative methods are equally profitable, at the maximum obtainable rate of profit, then the values of commodities will be indeterminate.

V. No matter how many alternative methods of production there may be, employing fixed capital or not and producing (pure) joint products or not, the von Neumann analysis determines, at a high level of abstraction, the profit rate, the growth rate, all prices of production, the allocation of labour, the choice of production methods, the economic life of capital goods and the pattern of outputs, in terms of the physically specified alternative production methods and the real wage bundle.[1] That determination involves no reference whatsoever to Marx's concept of value.

VI. The von Neumann analysis may be supplemented by Morishima's demonstration that the profit rate and growth rate are positive if and only if surplus labour, *as newly defined by Morishima*, is positive. This demonstration, again, requires no reference at all to Marx's concept of value.

VII. The effects of changes in the working day, of speed-up in the labour process, of increased pressure to save material inputs, etc., can be analysed within the physical quantities framework.

VIII. Given the physically specified methods of production and the *various* physically specified real wage rates, heterogeneous labour can readily be introduced into the determination of the rate of profit (and prices of production). It can also be shown how the existence of

---

[1] Some of these quantities may not be determined *uniquely* but the rates of profit and growth certainly will be (under the 'Fujimoto assumption').

profit is related to the performance of surplus labour. In neither case is there any need to 'reduce' one kind of labour-time to another.

IX. The rate of profit:

i) is not, in general, equal to total surplus value divided by the sum of total constant capital and total variable capital $(S/C+V)$ – the latter ratio provides no adequate measure of either the rate of profit in a capitalist economy or the potential for accumulation in such an economy;

ii) can fall only if real wages rise (relative to the hours and 'intensity' of work) and/or the conditions of production become technically less favourable;

iii) cannot be said *a priori* to have any prevailing tendency to move in one direction rather than the other.

Every part of each of the nine propositions just stated is claimed to follow inevitably from precise assumptions. Short of demonstrative proof that the claim is ill-founded, there are only three possible ways in which to respond to any one of those propositions:

a) to accept the proposition;

b) to reject *explicitly* one or more of the assumptions from which it is logically deduced;

c) to descend into obscurantism.

Of the first response, nothing need be said; while if the second be adopted, further discussion must necessarily depend on just which assumption is *explicitly* rejected. The third response, it need hardly be said, must be firmly resisted, whether it take one of the forms discussed in chapter 1 or any other form.

A brief assessment

A reasoned assessment of the implications of the Sraffa-based critique of Marx will, by its very nature, involve neither an iconoclastic dismissal of Marx's entire political economy nor a complacent conclusion that nothing of significance within that political economy need be changed. The Sraffa-based critique does indeed have significant implications for Marx's work but it does not entail a sweeping rejection of the entire edifice.

Thus, at the most general level, that critique is in no way destructive of the project of providing a materialist account of the capitalist mode of production; nor is it in the least inconsistent with the attempt to build a fully articulated social, political and economic account of particular capitalist social formations. More specifically, many aspects of Marx's political economy, because they are independent of his reasoning in terms of value magnitudes, are unaffected by the Sraffa-based critique. For example, the concepts of labour, of labour power and of surplus labour are quite untouched by that critique. So are Marx's emphases on the labour process, on coercion therein, and on the everchanging nature of the labour process resulting from both workplace conflicts and the competitive struggle. Equally unquestioned is Marx's stress on accumulation, involving both quantitative expansion and qualitative developments. Again, as was pointed out in chapter 1 (note 18), Marx's analysis of fetishism, reification and related matters is quite untouched by the Sraffa-based critique. That critique, which provides a definitive solution to only a particular range of issues, leaves open for investigation all the difficult problems relating, for example, to money, to effective demand and to crises; or to concentration, oligopoly and monopoly; or to the role of the state. Such investigation will no doubt draw on – amongst other sources – Marx's many insights which were independent of his value magnitude reasoning. It will be found that there is much in Marx's political economy which is unaffected by the Sraffa-based critique.

One must recognize equally clearly, however, that that critique is concerned with central issues within Marx's work. On the basis of assumptions to be found in Marx's own political economy, it has been proved that Marx's value reasoning is often internally inconsistent, completely failing to provide the explanations which Marx sought for certain central features of the capitalist economy. By contrast, these same features can be given a coherent explanation in terms which make no reference whatsoever to any value magnitude. Marx's value reasoning – hardly a peripheral aspect of his work – must therefore be abandoned, in the interest of developing a coherent materialist theory of capitalism.

Some of the elements of such a theory are to be found within the Sraffa-based critique itself. It has been shown that the proximate determinants of the rate of profit, the rate of accumulation, the prices of production, the social allocation of labour, etc. are the physical conditions of production, the real wage and the capitalist drive to accumulate. The next step then is to investigate the social, economic, political, technical, etc. determinants of those proximate determinants.[2] That immense task will perhaps involve the study of, *amongst other things*, the historical conditions under which specific capitalist social formations developed, class relations (both at the point of production and at the level of politics), the role of trades unions, the role of the state, the development of scientific and technical knowledge (considered not as a *deus ex machina* but as an endogenous product of the society in question) and international relations. Such study can no doubt draw on much of Marx's work, as one source amongst the many which will be needed. But *it will involve no reference to Marx's value magnitudes*, which are mere derivates of the things to be explained. It can scarcely be over-emphasized that the project of providing a materialist account of capitalist societies is dependent on Marx's value magnitude analysis *only* in the negative sense that continued adherence to the latter is a major fetter on the development of the former.

---

[2] It is not implied that all the relevant determinations must be uni-directional.

Appendix

Marx on Value, Money and Price

In this appendix a number of passages from Marx's work, relating to his interpretation of value, of money and of price, are drawn together in order to indicate what that interpretation was: no attempt will be made to provide a full *assessment*. More specifically, the following passages establish that the interpretation of the 'magnitude of value' and of the 'gold price' adopted in the text above is indeed to be found in Marx's writings.

Value

Consider first the following quotations concerning value.[1]

One. '. . . [abstracting from the useful character of the products of labour] they are merely congealed quantities of homogeneous human labour, i.e. of human labour-power expended without regard to the form of its expenditure . . . As crystals of this social substance, which is common to them all, they are values – commodity values.' (p. 128)

Two. 'A use-value, or useful article, therefore, has value only because abstract human labour is objectified or materialized in it. How, then, is the magnitude of this value to be measured? By means of the quantity of the "value-forming substance", the labour, con-

---

[1] Except where otherwise stated, all quotations are from *Capital*, vol. I, Penguin/NLR edition, 1976, to which the page references refer.

tained in the article. This quantity is measured by its duration, and the labour-time is itself measured on the particular scale of hours, days etc.' (p. 129)

Three. '. . . the labour that forms the substance of value . . .' (p. 129)

Four. 'What exclusively determines the magnitude of the value of any article is therefore the amount of labour socially necessary, or the labour-time socially necessary for its production.' (p. 129)

Five. 'Now we know the *substance* of value. It is *labour*. We know the *measure of its magnitude*. It is *labour-time*. The *form* . . . remains to be analysed.' (p. 131)

Six. '. . . the values coat and linen, however, are merely congealed quantities of homogeneous labour.' (pp. 135–6)

Seven. '. . . the magnitude of the value of a commodity represents nothing but the quantity of labour embodied in it . . .' (p. 136)

Eight. '. . . as values, commodities are simply congealed quantities of human labour . . .' (p. 141)

Nine. 'Human labour-power in its fluid state, or *human labour*, creates value, but is not itself value. It *becomes value in its coagulated state*, in objective form.' (p. 142, emphases added)

Ten. 'Here, as occasionally also on previous pages, we use the expression "value" for quantitatively determined values, i.e. for the magnitude of value.' (p. 145, n. 20)

Eleven. 'It is thus that this value first shows itself as being, in reality, a congealed quantity of undifferentiated human labour.' (p. 155)

Twelve. 'The same value, i.e. the same quantity of objectified social labour . . .' (p. 260)

Thirteen. 'The value of labour-power can be resolved into the value of a definite quantity of the means of subsistence. It therefore varies with the value of the means of subsistence, i.e. with the quantity of labour-time required to produce them.' (p. 276)

Fourteen. 'The maximum loss of value the means of production can suffer in the [labour] process is plainly limited by the amount of the original value with which they entered into it, or, in other words, by the labour-time required to produce them.' (pp. 313–14)

Fifteen. 'It is just as important for a correct understanding of surplus-value to conceive it as merely a congealed quantity of surplus labour-time, as nothing but objectified surplus labour, as it is for a proper comprehension of value in general to conceive it as merely a congealed quantity of so many hours of labour, as nothing but objectified labour.' (p. 325)

Sixteen. 'The value of labour-power, i.e. the labour-time necessary to produce labour-power . . .' (p. 430)

Seventeen. 'But what is the value of a commodity? The objective form of the social labour expended in its production. And how do we measure the quantity of this value? By the quantity of the labour contained in it.' (p. 675)

Eighteen. 'When commodities are exchanged in the proportion in which they represent equal amounts of labour-time, then it is their aspect as materialised labour-time, as embodied labour-time, which manifests their *substance*, the *identical element* they contain. As such, they are *qualitatively* the same, and differ only *quantitatively*, according to whether they represent smaller or larger quantities of the *same* substance, i.e. labour-time. They are *values* as expressions of the same element; and they are equal values, *equivalents*, insofar as they represent an equal amount of labour-time. They can only be compared as magnitudes, because they are already homogeneous magnitudes, qualitatively identical.

It is as manifestations of this substance that these different things constitute *values* and are related to one another as values; their different *magnitudes of value*, their immanent measure of value are thus also given. And only *because of this* can the value of a commodity be represented, expressed, in the use-values of other commodities as its equivalents. Hence the *individual commodity* as *value*, as the *embodiment of this substance*, is different from itself as use-value, as an object, quite apart from the expression of its value in other commodities. As the embodiment of labour-time, it is *value* in general, as the embodiment of a definite quantity of labour-time, it is a definite *magnitude of value*.'[2]

[2] *Theories of Surplus Value*, Part III, London, 1972, pp. 127–8.

It being understood then that the object of discussion is a capitalist, commodity producing economy, 'co-ordinated' through money flows in markets, and that only socially-necessary, *abstract social* labour, of average skill and intensity is referred to, it may be said that the 'magnitude of value' is a quantity of embodied labour-time. That this statement accurately reflects Marx's position cannot be altered by pointing to the fact that Marx was much concerned with the 'form of value', with the nature of 'abstract social' labour and with the 'universal equivalent'.

Money and price
Having emphasized that the magnitude of value is, for Marx, a quantity of embodied labour-time, one is, of course, obliged to explain at once his many statements in which the value of a commodity is expressed as an amount of money. The explanation is not hard to find and turns crucially on the word 'expressed'. In much, although not all, of his writing on money, Marx referred to a produced commodity money – gold – with its own 'magnitude of value' in the fundamental sense of a quantity of embodied, abstract social labour per physical unit of gold. In exchanging with a specific quantity of gold (its gold 'price'), one unit of any commodity, with its own value, is exchanged for another, special, commodity – the universal equivalent – which again has its own value. If all commodities, including the money commodity, exchange in proportion to their values (quantities of embodied, abstract social labour-time), then to say that a commodity has a particular price is an indirect way of saying that it has a particular value in the fundamental sense. Or, socially, the value of the commodity is *expressed* in its price. It is for this reason that Marx often refers to the value of a commodity as a quantity of *money* (gold), even though the fundamental meaning of the term refers to a quantity of socially necessary, abstract social *labour-time*. (As may be seen from quotation 24, Marx on occasion used *both* senses of 'value' in the same sentence!)
Nineteen. 'Throughout this work I assume that gold is the money

commodity, for the sake of simplicity.' (p. 188)

Twenty. 'The value, i.e. the quantity of human labour, which is contained in a ton of iron is expressed by an imaginary quantity of the money commodity which contains the same amount of labour as the iron'. (p. 190)

Twenty-one. 'The price of the commodity, therefore, is merely the money-name of the quantity of social labour objectified in it.' (p. 202)

Twenty-two. '. . . the values of commodities remaining constant, their prices vary with the value of gold (the material of money), rising in proportion as it falls, and falling in proportion as it rises.' (p. 213)

Twenty-three. 'Henceforth we shall assume the value of gold as a given factor . . .' (p. 214)

Twenty-four. 'It is true that the value of money varies, whether as a result of a variation in its own value, or of a change in the values of commodities.' (p. 230)

Twenty-five. '[Gold is] the directly social incarnation of all human labour.' (p. 230)

Twenty-six. 'The cotton originally bought for £100 is for example re-sold at £100 + £10 . . . This increment or excess over the original value I call "surplus-value".' (p. 251)

Twenty-seven. 'In this price [of 10 shillings] the labour required for the production of the cotton is already expressed in terms of average social labour.' (p. 293)

Twenty-eight. '. . . 12 shillings, i.e. the materialization of two days of labour.' (p. 295)

Twenty-nine. 'If 1 hour of work is embodied in sixpence, and the value of a day's labour-power is 5 shillings, the worker must work for 10 hours a day in order to replace the value paid by capital for his labour-power . . .' (p. 430)

Thirty. 'If 1 hour's labour is embodied in 6d., a value of 6s. will be produced in a working day of 12 hours.' (p. 433)

Thirty-one. '. . . a direct exchange of money, i.e. of objectified labour . . .' (p. 676)

Thirty-two. '. . . labour which creates a value of 6 shillings possesses a value of 3 shillings.' (p. 680)

Thirty-three. 'This reduction to simple, average labour is not, however, the only determinant of the *quality* of this labour to which as a unity the values of the commodities are reduced. That the quantity of labour embodied in a commodity is the quantity *socially necessary* for its production – the labour-time being thus *necessary labour-time* – is a definition which concerns only the *magnitude of value*. But the labour which constitutes the substance of value is not only uniform, simple, average labour; it is the labour of a private individual represented in a definite product. However, the product as value must be the embodiment of *social* labour and, as such, be directly convertible from one use-value into all others. (The particular use-value in which labour is directly represented is irrelevant so that it can be converted from one form into another). Thus the *labour of individuals* has to be directly represented as its opposite, *social* labour; this transformed labour is, as its immediate opposite, *abstract, general labour*, which is therefore represented in a general equivalent. Only by its alienation does individual labour manifest itself as its opposite. The commodity, however, must have this general expression before it is alienated. This necessity to express individual labour as general labour is equivalent to the necessity of expressing a commodity as money. The commodity receives this expression insofar as the money serves as a measure and expresses the value of the commodity in its *price*. It is only through sale, through its real transformation into money, that the commodity acquires its adequate expression as exchange-value.'[3]

[3] *Ibid.*, pp. 135–6.

Name Index

This index contains no entries for either Marx or Sraffa.

Subject Index

wages 92–3, 100–3, 204; and
heterogeneous labour 92–3, 100–3
'Reduction' of skilled to unskilled
labour redundant 91, 92, 93,
204–5
Rent 13n
Reproduction of both social
relations and means of
production 18–19, 20

Savings assumptions; workers save
nothing *passim*, capitalists save all
their profits 99, 150–62, 187–201
Socialist planning, irrelevance of
embodied labour-times to 112n
Surplus labour, as defined by
Morishima 192–4, 198–200, 204,
206
Surplus value, additive 37, 41, 48,
55, 154; positively related to
profits 34–5, 57, 172–3, 203; that
positive relation *not* a theory of
profit 57–9, 203; can be
negatively related to profit 154;
and heterogeneous labour 88–94,
179
'Surrogate' production function
106n, 108n

Technical composition of capital –
see Value composition of capital
Technical progress 117, 128–9,
129n, 131, 200
'Transformation problem' 29–36;
Marx's solution invalid 14, 29–31,
43–4; a pseudo-problem 14, 52,
56; 'transformation' of input
prices 31–3, 43–4
Turnover problems 103–5, 112–15,
124, 181–3

Value composition of capital 37,
106–8, 119; and technical
progress 117; alleged tendency to
rise 117–25; and other

'compositions of capital' 132–6;
negative 156
Value magnitudes, additive;
continued adherence to, a major
fetter on the materialist project
207; dependent on the wage when
there is a choice of production
methods 65, 147–8; derivative
nature of 56–7, 59, 65, 66–7, 138,
202; determination of 55, 118,
138–46, 154, 165; irrelevance of
15, 26, 27, 52, 57, 59, 64–5, 65n,
67, 111–12, 114, 136, 146–7, 149,
162, 170, 172, 178, 183, 194, 197,
198, 199, 200–1, 204, 206–7;
labour-time and 20, 39–40, 60–1,
83n, 208–11; values can be
negative 145–6, 154, 165, 165n,
203; 'value depreciation' 138–46,
148–9; value magnitudes
determine the *physical* form of the
surplus but *not* the specifically
capitalist form of that surplus
109–11; values as 'employment
multipliers' 157–9; value of an
'old' machine can exceed that of a
'new' one 144
Value of labour power 37, 41, 48,
55, 74, 120, 154, 174; with
heterogeneous labour (the V
matrix) 91–2, 93–4, 179
'Value rate of profit' $(S/C + V)$; not
equal to the actual rate of profit
14, 30–1, 44, 46–9, 61, 96–8, 172,
173–5, 198n, 205; its irrelevance
30, 99, 99n, 205

Wage-profit frontier 106, 127–8,
191, 197n
Wage rate and rate of exploitation
105–9
Wages; discussed 20–1; pre- or
post-payment of 21, 21n, 79n,
103–5, 189n; timing of wage
payments 103–5